LOYALIST FOODS

in

TODAY'S RECIPES

by
Eleanor Robertson Smith

ISBN 1-895991-08-0

Published 1983

Seventh printing 2000

Copyright© 2000
Shelburne County Genealogical Society
PO Box 248 Shelburne, Nova Scotia B0T1W0

Printed by
Sentinel Printing
14 Kirk St. Yarmouth, NS

4

LOYALIST FOODS
in
TODAY'S RECIPES

CONTENTS

ACKNOWLEDGEMENTS

Grateful acknowledgement is made to the Royal Canadian Geographical Society who provided a research grant and to the members of the following organizations all of whom helped me in my research:

Shelburne County Museum, Shelburne Historical Society, Public Archives of Nova Scotia, Public Archives of Canada, Nova Scotia Museum, Acadia University Rare Book Library, University of Manitoba Library, New Brunswick Museum, Collections of the New Brunswick Historical Society, Collections of the New York Historical Society.

A special thanks to Marion Robertson who provided me with information and encouragement; and to my husband Jim, my son Greg, and my 86 year old dad, Lew Robertson who tasted and helped me refine the recipes.

I appreciate the many who contributed recipes: Mrs. Amy Bower, Mrs. John Cann, Doreen Craton, Mrs. Millard Fillmore, Gertrude Fillmore, Olive Flatt, Pauline Goodspeed, Thelma Grovestine, Cathy Hay, Shirley Hilchie, Yvette Harris, Ken O'Brien, Mrs. Mary Malowsky, Diane Oades, Ruby Perry, and Catherine Thomas.

I also acknowledge thanks to the artists John David Smith and Joseph Lewis for the illustrations commissioned especially for this book; to my daughter Andrea, for the facisimiles of letters and court records; to my daughter and son-in-law Roxanne and Terry Carter for testing recipes; to my typist, Barb Bissell, and to Mary Archibald, Finn Bower, Rita Bower, Sally Cranston, Lila Goodspeed, Mike Luik, Barbara Robertson, Isobel Wettlaufer and others for assistance with this endeavour.

Copyright excerpts have been reprinted with the permission of:

Mary Archibald, Shelburne Historical Society, Public Archives of Nova Scotia, New Brunswick Historical Society, Dundurn Press, Cherry Tree Press.

6

DEDICATION

To my United Empire Loyalist ancestors:

Corporal John and Margaret (Hauphman) Robertson
John and Jennet McDonald
Captain James and Anna (McGeorge) Hamilton
Alexander and Agnes (Hamilton) Hogg
William and Sarah (Tinkler) Moses

INTRODUCTION

Rediscover the fascinating foodways of 200 years ago as gleaned from diaries, letters, day books, yellow fragile pages, motley shades of browned ink, strange scripts, graceful handwriting and forgotten but descriptive phraseology. These aged sources augmented with newspaper collections from Public Archives and early cookbooks provided the background for this book.

"Receipts", as they were called in the late eighteenth century, are interesting to read but impossible to prepare without adaption. Commercial baking powder and baking soda were non-existent; eggs were pullet size; poultry and domesticated animals roamed for their own food developing muscles which required extended periods of cooking; flours, grains and sugars were much coarser than today.

This recipe collection, uses the foods consumed by the Loyalists, retains the early herb, spice and culinary combinations, has passed the test of time and has been tested and re-tested to provide you with delicious recipes for today.

It is hoped the reader of this book will enjoy an adventure in healthful eating spiced with bits of the social history of the Maritime Loyalist settlers.

The Way It Was...an Era of Extremities

Captain William Booth, a Royal Engineer posted at Shelburne from 1787-1789, wrote six small booklets of what he termed "Rough Memorandums". Like most diarists he described the weather using the in vogue idioms such as: "tolerable fine; thick and nasty weather; hard frost, water in the chamber froze for the first time this winter".[1]

Feb. 5, 1789

Current prices for provisions at Shelburne.

Beef 5 shillings .... Butter 1
Veal 7 1/2 .... Sugar 10
Mutton None .... Tea, good souching 10
A string of trout as many as might serve 2 moderate people
4
A loaf of bread as much as Graves, Mrs. B and myself eat a
day 3
Rum excellent 5 of indifferent quality 4
Very good maderia wine 7/6
Port at the same price

June 12, 1789
Cod (enough for 3 people) 5 coppers
Salmon, weighing 12 pounds 1/3
A set of calves feet 6
Fowls 7 1/2
Partridges, excellent, (3 per brace) 1
2 braces of ducks 2[2]

Game, a valued food was frequently peddled from door to door or sold in the public meat market.

March 26, 1789
The people about the country have been very successful in moose hunting, they have killed upwards of a hundred. A good deal of that meat has been brought to the Shelburne Market.
It sold for 1 to 6 and is of great help to the poorer sort of the inhabitants, indeed the meat is so good that everyone has a desire to partake of some of it. I had as tender a steak today of that meat as ever I would wish to eat, it was only in want of fat. Moose meat makes excellent soup.[3]

Hannah Booth, his wife, died after a lingering illness and is buried in a Shelburne cemetery. In a letter to her brother Booth related

March 17, 1789
Dr. recommended Veal broth, Calves feet, and such

nourishing Foods as she should be inclined to eat — Veal and veal soup we were never without, and usually had good mutton in the house, but the calves feet for jelly we could not always obtain.[4]

After Hannah's funeral Booth moved out of their house and rented three rooms from Mrs. Holderness, the wife of a merchant who frequently sailed to the West Indies on business. Booth described the house as large and "the second or third best in town". His rooms consisted of a bedchamber upstairs, a front parlour, use of the kitchen and a garret for his three servants (two "black girls" and his "man Graves"). He paid rent weekly at 18 per annum and supplied the kitchen with fuel from his rations.

March 13 Private Memorandum
My cough is getting better as the weather becomes milder. I take honey on toast with butter in the morning and in the afternoon on bread and butter. Drink Licorice boiled in water and a little weak broth at 12'o'clock in the day. Eat a very moderate dinner, mutton hot and cold when I can get it, the latter with oil and vinegar. Seldom drink more than 2 glasses of wine being well chosen maderia. Never eat suppers.

March 22, 1789
Having had a goose brought to me which I purchased for 3/9/ / by Mrs. Holderness I requested her to do me the honour of partaking of it with two of her children. They dined with me today. Gave Veal Soup Cranberry Tart with apples, nuts and some sweetmeats. They took tea and departed at 8 in the evening. She appears a pleasant woman...daughters fine at the table.[5]

August 1, 1789
If Mr. Martens' should be disengaged tomorrow Captain Booth will be glad of his company at dinner tomorrow.[6]

Sept. 30
Scarcity of flour complained of in Town; the Bakers say they have none to supply their customers.[7]

August 14
Mr. McMaster sent me some remarkable fine pease and

11

beans the other day — sent in return my compliments and begged his acceptance of a couple of Tongues.[6]

In the Tuesday August 26, 1783 entry of his diary, Benjamin Marston, the first surveyor of Shelburne related a breach of etiquette:

> ...just after I came home received a billet from Captain Christian inviting me to see him on board the *Cyclops* this afternoon or tomorrow at breakfast. Sent a verbal answer I would breakfast with him. I was too tired, too dirty,too hungry to sit down and write an answer to his billet. He may think me an odd fellow; he is welcome to his opinion.
>
> Sunday, Oct. 5th Dined on board the *Cyclops* in the Gun Room. Noise and Nonsence.
> Monday, Oct. 6th Dined on board ditto, in the Great Cabin —decency & agreeableness[8]

Shipboard dining and dancing were popular at each of the Loyalist port towns. A present-day artist, Joseph Lewis, depicts a cabin supper scene aboard the *Andromeda*. In 1787, Prince William, who later became William IV, was stationed in Halifax as commander of the *Andromeda*. His "bosom friend" was William Dyott, a British officer on garrison duty in Halifax. Dyott kept a detailed diary which provides interesting descriptions of Nova Scotia and the social life of that period. The Prince frequently entertained aboard the *Andromeda* providing a "superb dinner" or an evening of dancing followed by supper:

> The ladies went below, and the colors that divided the quarter-deck were drawn up in festoons and displayed the most completely elegant supper I ever saw. At the end of the deck were two transparent paintings, the one representing the Scottish motto and thistle, the other St. George's Cross and Garter. Upwards of sixty people sat down to supper at a table almost in the form of a horse-shoe. The supper was chiefly cold, except soups and removes,* with partridges, etc.,champage, hock,

* removes — see glossary

etc. In Short the whole was by far the most elegant thing I ever saw. We remained more than an hour at supper....[9]   (See page 8)

Elaborate dinner parties were frequently held by government officials and military officers. Newspapers give glowing accounts of birthday celebrations honouring royalty, feasts honouring patron saints and formal fraternal repasts. *The Royal Gazette and New Brunswick Advertiser,* St. John, Feb. 21, 1786 contains a report, from a Halifax correspondent, which describes the January 20th birthday celebration held at Halifax in honour of Queen Charlotte:

> The evening was concluded by a splendid ball at Roubatils...At the close of the fifth country dance supper was announced, in a most romantic manner, by the sudden elevation of a curtain that separated the two rooms, and displayed to the enraptured beholder, a complete masterpiece of pastry work. In the middle of the table sprung up an artificial fountain in defiance of the frost itself; and on each side in proper distances were erected pyramids, obelisks, and monuments — with the temples of Health and Venus at the top and bottom. During the course of the repast, the music attended to delight the ear and please the more delicate senses, while the great variety of the most exquisite served to gratify the palate.

In contrast to the gay time of some inhabitants, the poor of the towns suffered and even died from the lack of the necessities of life. The Shelburne County Court Records give unbelievable details of Catherine Smith dying from the want of food. She was a "pauper in the poor house who was subject to fits". The court testimony reveals that the regular weekly poor rations were: three quarts of Indian meal, a pint of molasses, three ounces of salt fish and six quarts of potatoes. Since Catherine was ailing the keeper requested permission to give her some fresh provisions in place of the salt fish. The next week the salt fish was discontinued but no fresh provisions were provided. Instead the Indian meal was increased to four quarts. This ration continued for three weeks. For the two days before her death there was no food available. When Dr. Perry took the witness stand he told of two visits to Catherine. The first time he advised she be given gruel and stated that at that time she had no blanket, no gown nor shift, no cap, no straw to lie on and that he requested the latter for her. He believed "her Death was hastened by want of the common necessities of life".[10]

Boston King, a Black Loyalist happily described an increase in his winter supplies:

> ...and my Winter's store consisted of one barrel of flour, three bushels of corn, nine gallons of treacle, 20 bushels of potatoes which my wife had set in my absence, and two barrels of fish; so that was the best Winter I ever saw in Burchtown.[11]

Soon after the towns were founded there was evidence of legislation enacted to protect resources and the consumer. Salmon, which had been depleted from many of the New England streams before the Loyalists left the colonies were protected in a number of ways. Salmon fry could not be sold in the fish market; salmon nets could cover only one-third of a stream; the days and hours of setting and lifting nets were regulated; scoup nets were forbidden at or above the falls of any rivers; slabs and other refuse from mills were to be retained on the land. It is interesting to note that one-half of the fines collected from offenders were given to the informer and the other half were appropriated towards clearing the rivers of incumbrances. Flour and bread were examined by government inspectors for adulteration; weights were checked regularly and the prices for board and lodging at travens and coffee houses were regulated. *The Royal American Gazette*, Shelburne, March 18, 1784 stated:

> For a Man, or a Woman, Breakfast of Bread, Butter, Tea, Coffee, or Chocolate, with Loaf Sugar — Six Pence
> A Servant, Breakfast — Four Pence
> For a Man, or Woman's Dinner of good Wholesome

Meat, with Bread, and Vegetables — Ten Pence
A Servant's Dinner — Six Pence
For a Man, or Woman's Supper of Good Wholesome
Meat with Bread, and Vegetables — Eight Pence.
A Servant's Supper — Five Pence
For Man, or Woman's Tea, or Coffee, in the
Afternoon, with Bread, Butter, and Loaf Sugar —
Eight Pence
Man, or Woman's Breakfast, or Supper of Bread, and
Milk, —Four Pence.

Alexander Huston — whose diary tells not only of his having laboured hard each day cutting wood and clearing the land of stumps so that he could plant potatoes, barley and buckwheat, but also notes such events as his wife Jenny's daily trips to deliver milk to the Barracks and the visits of various tradespeople — has summed up the marvellous spirit or our forefathers in these entries:

> Tuesday December 25 (1787). A mixture of snow and rain. Wind at NW. Children bad with sore throats and a cold. Yet we did spend Christmas very agreeably more so than any I can remember. The weather is amazing Good and the most open season I ever did see in America.

> and on December 31, (1787)
> ....this ends this year in which I may say I have been wonderfully provided for by infinite providence; this year the crops failed much. Being a late cold spring and a wet summer and very early frost in autumn. But an exceeding fine fall and moderate winter....[12]

Our Loyalist heritage reflects the extremities of life: adversity and thankfulness; hard work and frivolity; the wealthy and the poor; plenty and scarcity; and always ingenuity and acceptance.

Now delight in the legacy of the Loyalists and partake in this adventure of wholesome fare!

SOUPS AND CHOWDERS

JS'83

The kitchen hearth in the cellar of the Ross Thomson House, Shelburne, N.S. (1785-   ).

SOUPS AND CHOWDERS

In early Nova Scotian homes, the iron "chaudiere" or soup kettle was usually filled with a simmering soup or stock. Sometimes the kettle was suspended over the fire by an S-shaped hook attached to a movable crane, but at other times the kettle was placed directly on the hearth. Three supporting feet kept the pot raised above the embers, and adjusted to the uneven cooking surfaces.

Soups were made in great variety, and cook book authorities gave many general directions and rules for soup-making.

Every particle of fat should be carefully skimmed from the surface. Greasy soup is disgusting and unwholesome.[1]

To send the soup to the table with bits of bone and shreds of meat in it, is a slovenly, disgusting and vulgar practice, and should be strictly forbidden; as some indifferent cooks will do so to save themselves the trouble of removing it.[2]

When soups or gravies are to be put by, let them be changed every day into fresh scalded pans. Whatever has vegetables in it, is apt to turn sooner than juices of meat. Never keep any gravy in metal...
Long boiling is necessary to give the full flavour of the ingredients, therefore time should be allowed for soups and gravies; and they are best if made the day before they are wanted...
A clear jelly of cow-heels is very useful to keep in the house, being a great improvement to soups and gravies.[3]

The third stock, being made from bones and pieces of meat left from roasts, and from the trimmings of raw meats, will always be changeable in color, quantity and quality. This is, however, a very important stock, and it should always be kept on hand. No household, even where only a moderate amount of meat is used, should be without a stock-pot. It can be kept on the back of the range or stove while cooking is going on. Two or three times a week it should be put on with the

19

trimmings and bones left from cooked and uncooked meats. This practice will give a supply of stock at all times, which will be of the greatest value in making sauces, side dishes and soups. Meat, if only slightly tainted, will spoil a stock; therefore great care must be taken that every particle is perfectly sweet. Vegetables make a stock sour very quickly, so if you wish to keep a stock do not use them. Many rules advise putting vegetables into the stock-pot with the meat and water, and cooking from the very beginning. When this is done they absorb the fine flavour of the meat and give the soup a rank taste. They should cook not more than an hour — the last hour in the stock.[4]

Portable or "pocket soup" was used by travellers, soldiers, woodsmen, and seafarers. When dried, the cakes were stored in tin boxes with a piece of paper between each cake. The next time you reach for a bouillon cube think of the effort involved in preparing this recipe.

PORTABLE SOUP

Boil one or two knuckles of veal, one or two shins of beef, in as much water only as will cover them. Take the marrow out of the bones, put any sort of spice you like, and three large onions. When the meat is done to rags, strain it off, and put it into a very cold place. When cold, take off the cake of fat (which will make crusts for servants' pies), put the soup into a double-bottomed tin sauce-pan, and set it on a pretty quick fire, but don't let it burn. It must boil fast and uncovered, and be stirred constantly for eight hours. Put it into a pan, and let it stand in a cold place a day; then pour it into a round soup china-dish, and set the dish into a stew-pan of boiling water on a stove, and let it boil, and be now and then stirred, till the soup is thick and ropy; then it is enough. Pour it into the little round part at the bottom of cups or basins turned upside down, to form cakes; and when cold, turn them out on flannel to dry. Keep them in tin canisters. When they are to be used, melt them in boiling water; and if you wish the flavour of herbs, or anything else, boil it first, strain off the water, and melt the soup in it.
This is very convenient in the country, or at sea, where fresh meat is not always at hand; as by this means a basin of soup may be made in five minutes.[5]

CLAM CHOWDER

Clam chowder had been an Atlantic coast specialty since the early days of settlement. This modern recipe for clam chowder is followed by an 1852 "receipt".

1/2 cup	bacon or salt pork	125mL
3 cups	shucked clams	750mL
	or	
2 cans	clams	2
1	onion, diced	1
3	medium potatoes, cubed	3
2 cups	clam juice	500mL
3 cups	whole milk	750mL
1 can	evaporated milk	385mL
	or	
1 1/2 cups	cereal cream	375mL
2 tablespoons	butter	30mL
1/2 teaspoon	thyme	2mL
1/2 teaspoon	oregano	2mL
	freshly ground pepper	
	salt	

1. Fresh clams: Discard black part of neck. Chop remaining pieces. Strain clam liquor through a sieve, with double thickness of cheese cloth, set over a bowl.
   Canned clams: mince bodies. Drain and save liquor.
2. Cut the bacon or salt pork in small pieces and fry until crisp. Transfer to a paper towel.
3. Add onion to the pan and saute until transparent. Pour off excess fat. Add potatoes, oregano, thyme, and clam juice. Cook until potatoes are almost tender. Add minced clams and simmer 5 minutes longer.
4. Add milk, bacon and freshly ground pepper. Taste for salt. Heat until hot, but do not boil as curdling will take place. Ladle into heated bowls. Place 1 teaspoon butter on top of each serving.

Yields: 5 servings

My great-great grandparents, Michael and Jennet McDonald Robertson* ran a successful hostel on Robertson's Hill in Port Joli, Queen's Country. Jennet's copy of the popular *Miss Eliza Leslie's*

*both Loyalist descendants

New Receipts For Cooking has remained in the family. Here is Miss Leslie's receipt for Excellent Clam Soup. (p. 14).

EXCELLENT CLAM SOUP

Take forty or fifty clams, and wash and scrub the outsides of the shells till they are perfectly clean. Then put them into a pot with just sufficient water to keep them from burning. The water must boil hard when you put in the clams. In about a quarter of an hour the shells will open, and the liquor run out and mix with the water, which must be saved for the soup, and strained into a soup-pot after the clams are taken out. Extract the clams from their shells, and cut them up small. Then put them into the soup-pot, adding a minced onion, a saucer of finely chopped celery, or a table-spoonful of celery seed, and a dozen blades of mace, with a dozen whole pepper-corns. No salt, as the clam liquor will be quite salt enough. If the liquid is not in sufficient quantity to fill a large tureen, add some milk. Thicken the soup with two large tablespoonfuls of fresh butter rolled in flour. Let it boil a quarter of an hour, or twenty minutes. Just before you take it from the fire, stir in, gradually, the beaten yolks of five eggs: and then take up the soup, and pour it into a tureen, the bottom of which is covered with toasted bread, cut into square dice about a inch in size.

OYSTER STEW

During my childhood oyster stew was a favourite Sunday supper dish. Dad annually ordered a barrel of oysters from a Bras d'Or Lake shipper. The barrel would arrive by train in October and the oysters would keep fresh in our cellar. This simple to make recipe is found in my maternal grandmother's copy of *Dr. Alvin Chase's Practical Recipes.* To adapt the recipe use one half cup of cereal cream for the gill of milk. Do not boil the ingredients once the cream is added.

To each dozen or dish of oysters put a half pint of water; milk 1 gill; butter $\frac{1}{2}$ oz.; powdered crackers to thicken. Bring the oysters and water to a boil, then add the other ingredients previously mixed together, and boil from 3 to 5 minutes only.

Each one will choose to add salt, pepper, &c., to their own taste. Keep about these proportions if you should have to cook for an oyster supper for parties, &c.(p. 58).

Port Roseway July 1. 1783

My stay here shall be very short but I will first look at the Fishery we went & returned well satisfied, Providence in this Article has been exceeding bountifull, fish never was more plenty nor easeyer come at, than from this place. Great numbers of Vessells from different places of New England are here fishing, which by the by was infamous in the Peace Makers to allow.

We have got our town Lott which is just large enough for a good House and Small Garden, and [   ].

Facsimilie excerpt of a letter written by James Courtney to Archibald Cunningham on arriving at Port Roseway. (P.A.N.S. White Collection of MSS #210)

Three years later an advertisement in *Royal American Gazette* Shelburne, N.S., July 13, 1786 states that James Courtney had a few very good Milch cows to be sold at Courtney's Mills so his stay was much longer then he envisaged.

SOUTH SHORE FISH CHOWDER

Versatile fish chowder is a popular way of serving the plentiful harvest from the sea.

4	medium potatoes, diced	4
2	onions, diced	2
1/2 cup	diced celery	125mL
1/2 cup	sliced carrot	125mL

1 1/2 pounds	haddock	0.75Kg
2 cans	evaporated milk	770mL
2 tablespoons	butter	30mL
	salt and pepper	

1. Melt butter in large saucepan and cook celery and onion in it until limp. Add potatoes, carrots, water to cover, salt and pepper. Simmer until vegetables are tender-crisp.
2. Cut haddock fillets in bite-sized pieces. Add to vegetables and cook 10 minutes longer.
3. Add milk. Re-heat but do not boil. Flavour improves if made an hour ahead of serving. This chowder freezes beautifully and is best reheated in a crock-pot or the top of a double boiler.

Serves: 6

LOBSTER CHOWDER

2 cups	cooked lobster	500mL
1	medium onion, chopped	1
2	medium potatoes, cubed	2
2 cups	whole milk	500mL
1 can	evaporated milk	385mL
2 tablespoons	butter	30mL
1 teaspoon	salt	5mL
1/4 teaspoon	pepper	1mL

1. Cook onion and potatoes in 1 cup (250mL) water. When nearly tender add cut-up lobster. Season with salt and pepper and simmer 5 minutes.
2. Add milk and butter, heat to just below the boiling point. Serve piping hot with crisp crackers.

Servings: 4

SEAFOOD CHOWDER

The medley varies according to the availability of seafoods and also to their affordability. Fresh, frozen, or canned fish can be used. The following recipe is one from my mother-in-law who was famous for her delectable chowders.

| 1 | medium onion, minced | 1 |

1	potato, diced	1
1 pound	scallops, sliced	0.5kg
2 pounds	haddock	1kg
1/2 cup	tiny clams, steamed	125mL
	or canned clams and juice	
1 cup	cooked or canned lobster	250mL
2 tablespoons	butter	30mL
1 can	evaporated milk	385mL
2 cups	whole milk	500mL
	salt and pepper	

1. Simmer onion and potato in small amount of water until tender crisp. Add cut up haddock and juice from clams and lobster. Cook 10 minutes.
2. Add clams, scallops and lobster meat (cut up). Simmer 5 minutes. Add butter, salt and pepper to taste.
3. Add milk and heat to just below boiling point. Always make chowder a couple of hours ahead and leave on stove or in crock pot to improve flavour.

Serves: 8

CLAM AND LEEK CHOWDER

An interesting combination of flavours is found in this hearty soup. Leeks, celery, marjoram, thyme and parsley were all grown in the gardens of Shelburne between 1785 and 1820.

1	medium onion, diced	1
2	leeks, diced	2
1/2 cup	celery, chopped	125mL
4	slices of bacon	4
	or	
2 tablespoons	butter	30mL
3 tablespoons	flour	45mL
1 can	clams	142g
	(and juice)	
2 1/2 cups	water	625mL
1/4 cup	ketchup	50mL
1/2 teaspoon	thyme	2mL
1/2 teaspoon	marjoram	2mL
1 tablespoon	chopped parsley	15mL
	salt and pepper	
1 can	evaporated milk	385mL

1. Cut bacon in small pieces and fry until crisp or melt butter.
2. Saute the diced vegetables in the fat until transparent. Add flour and mix well. Slowly add water and cook until vegetables are tender.
3. Add clams, and juice, ketchup, seasonings and heat until just below boiling point.
4. Add milk. Reheat, but do not boil. Taste for seasoning. Add finely chopped parsley and serve.

Servings: 6

EXCHANGE
COFFEE-HOUSE.

CHARLES M' PHERSON, begs leave to inform his friends and the public, that he has finished his house in the best manner for the reception of company.—He also begs leave to return his most sincere thanks to his friends, and the public in general, for their past favours, and hopes for a continuance of them ; as he will make it his constant study to give his customers every satisfaction in his power.—For the convenience of travellers he will have BREAKFASTS from 8 to 10 o'clock and SOUPS from 11 to 1 o'clock, DINNERS precisely at 2 o'clock and RELISHES on the shortest notice.— He has furnished himself with, and will constantly keep the best liquors in the province.

☞ Boarding and lodging by the week on the most reasonable terms.

The Royal Gazette and New Brunswick Advertiser carried the preceding advertisement in the September 5, 1786 edition. Note that soups were a daily feature between 11 and 1 o'clock while dinner was a more formal occasion being served precisely at 2 o'clock.

MULLIGATAWNY SOUP

This soup was brought from India by British soldiers who served there. It was a favourite with sea-faring men and one early cook book states it's a good way to utilize a "tough fowl." This present day version proves the soup merits years of popularity.

3-4 lb.	boiling fowl or	2kg
	utility chicken	
4	onions	4
4	carrots	4
3	celery stalks and leaves	3
1/4 cup	butter	50mL
1/4 cup	flour	50mL
1-2 tablespoons	curry powder	15-30mL
2	whole cloves	2
1 teaspooon	salt	5mL
1/8 teaspoon	nutmeg	0.5mL
1/4 teaspoon	thyme	1mL
1/2 cup	rice	125mL
1 cup	cereal cream	250mL
	parsley	

1. Place chicken in a saucepan with 7 cups (1.5L) of water. Add a peeled onion, a peeled and sliced carrot, and a celery stalk and celery leaves. Bring to a rolling boil, cover and simmer 1 hour or until chicken is tender.
2. Remove chicken from stock; cool and discard skin and bones. Dice meat and strain stock.
3. Put 1 cup (250mL) of stock in small saucepan. Add 1/2 teaspoon (2mL) salt and rice. Bring to boil, cover and let stand for 15 minutes.
4. Peel and chop remaining vegetables.* Melt butter in large saucepan, add vegetables and stir over low heat until tender crisp. Add seasonings and flour. Mix well.
5. Add stock and bring to a boil. Cover and simmer 30 minutes.
6. Check seasonings. Add cream and 2 cups (450mL) diced chicken. Heat gently, but do not boil.
7. Place a heaping spoon of rice in each soup bowl, add soup and garnish with snipped parsley.

Garnish: rice and parsley
Servings: 6

VEGETABLE SOUPS

In 1795, Reverend James Munroe toured the southern townships of Nova Scotia and wrote an extensive report on them. Here is his description of the kitchen gardens of Shelburne:

> ..In the Town are good gardens full of garden stuff. Roots, such as Turnip, carrot, parsenup, onions, and cabbage but the cabbage do not answer well by reason of grub or maggot that cuts them off at the root. Sallads as lattice, Beets, parcely, Raddish. There are cucumbers, pumpkins, squashes, Mush and watermellons. Berries such as gooseBerries raseberries and currants in the greatest abundance I ever saw and of the best quality peace and Beans of different kinds are found there. (p. 44)

The following recipes are the "stick to your ribs" variety which utilize some of the vegetables described by Reverend Munroe.

CHUNKY BEEF VEGETABLE SOUP

1	large soupbone (ask butcher to split*)	1
2 pounds	shin beef	1kg
4 quarts	water	4L
1 tablespoon	salt	15mL
1/2	medium cabbage, shredded	1/2
2	onions, chopped	2
6	carrots, pared and cut in 2 inch pieces	6
2	stalks celery, coarsely cut up	2
1 can	tomatoes	796mL
1 package	frozen mixed vegetables	907g
1/2 cup	barley	125mL
2 tablespoons	snipped parsley	30mL
3/4 cup	catchup	175mL
1 teaspoon	salt	5mL
1/2 teaspoon	pepper	2mL
1 teaspoon	worcestershire sauce	5mL

Day before:
1. In large kettle place meat, bone, water and salt.
2. Bring to boil. Skim.
* Cracking the bone allows more flavour, marrow and gelatine to be released.

28

3. Add cabbage, onions, carrots, celery, and tomatoes. Cook, covered, 30 minutes.
4. Add remainder of ingredients. Simmer, covered for 3 hours.
5. Taste for seasoning. Remove meat and bone from soup. Cut up meat and return to the soup.
6. Cool and then refrigerate to allow flavors to blend.

Next day:
1. Skim any fat from soup. Bring to boil over medium heat.
2. Simmer 5 minutes. Serve.

Servings: 12 Freezes well.

VEGETARIAN BORSCHT

2	carrots, peeled and sliced	2
1	potato, peeled and sliced	1
1	onion, peeled and sliced	1
4	beets, cooked, peeled, sliced	4
	or	
1 can	beets	680mL
1	stalk celery, scraped, sliced	1
1/2 cup	wax beans	125mL
1/4 cup	parsley, fresh, snipped	50mL
4	tomatoes	4
	or	
1 can	tomatoes	796mL
1 tablespoon	salt	15mL
1 tablespoon	sugar	15mL
1 tablespoon	lemon juice	15mL

1. Cook beets until tender, peel and slice.
2. Place potato, carrots, celery, onion, beahs, parsley in a large pot. Cover with water. Cover pot and cook until tender. Add prepared beets. Drain and save liquid.
3. Mash vegetables in pot. Return liquid to the vegetables.
4. Add tomatoes, salt, sugar and lemon juice. Simmer, covered for 30 minutes, adding just enough water to keep vegetables covered. Taste for seasoning.
5. Serve hot or cold.

Garnish: a dab of sour cream, minced dill
Servings: 6

MINESTRONE SOUP

4 tablespoons	butter	60mL
1	leek finely chopped	1
	or	
2	chopped onions	2
2	stalks celery, sliced	2
2 cups	diced, unpeeled cucumber	500mL
1 cup	peas, fresh or frozen	250mL
1 cup	diced carrots	250mL
1 cup	diced potatoes	250mL
1/2 teaspoon	minced garlic	2mL
2 cups	tomatoes, **coarsely** chopped	500mL
1	bay leaf	1
2 tablespoons	parsley	30mL
1/2 teaspoon	savory	2mL
1/2 teaspoon	marjoram	2 mL
1 teaspoon	salt	5mL
	freshly ground pepper	
1/2 cup	rice	125mL
2 quarts	chicken or vegetable stock	2L
1 cup	canned chick peas	250mL

1. Saute leek, celery, cucumber, carrots, and potatoes in butter and garlic.
2. Add tomatoes, peas, rice, broth, and seasonings. Bring to a boil and simmer, covered for 25 minutes.
3. Add chick peas. Reheat. Taste the soup and season. Garnish with parmesan cheese and serve.

Serves: 8
Garnish: Parmesan cheese

ONION SOUP GRATINEE

Gideon White, a **prominent** citizen and one of the founders of the town of Shelburne, frequently mentioned gardening activities in his day books. On April 17, 1795 he "Planted three beds onions."[6]

4	medium large onions	4
3 tablespoons	butter	45mL
6 cups	beef stock or bouillon cube broth	1.5L
1 teaspoon	salt	5mL
1/2 teaspoon	pepper	2mL

Day-old French bread (or toast)
Grated Parmesan cheese

1. Peel and slice the onions and cook very gently in butter. Cook only until transparent, not brown, to retain a delicate flavor.
2. Pour the stock over the onions and bring to the boiling point. Simmer about ten minutes and set aside to blend for a few hours.
3. To serve; heat to piping hot in casserole or onion soup bowls. Arrange slices of toasted bread on top and sprinkle the bread with grated cheese.
4. Return to hot oven just long enough to brown the cheese.

Servings: 4

TOMATO OR "LOVE APPLE" SOUP

A Nova Scotia Museum report on the *Gardens of Shelburne 1785-1820* lists about 60 herbs and vegetable seeds which were sold by the local seed merchants. "Love apple", the name sometimes used for tomatoes, is on the list.

Recipes for tomato soup in 18th and 19th century cookbooks always included a small amount of baking soda to prevent curdling. Today's cooks realize soda destroys the Vitamin C in tomatoes and that by slowly adding the hot tomato mixture to the heated milk the soup remains smooth.

1 can	tomatoes	796 mL
1	slice onion	1
1 teaspoon	sugar	5mL
1 teaspoon	salt	5mL
4	peppercorns	4
1/4 cup	butter	50mL
1/4 cup	flour	50mL
2 1/2 cups	milk	625mL
	crackers	

1. Simmer tomatoes, onion, sugar, salt and peppercorns about 8 minutes.
2. *Press* tomato mixture through a sieve into a bowl. (Discard seeds, peppercorn, onion)
3. Melt butter in saucepan, mix in flour, then add milk. Cook over

31

moderate heat until just below the boiling point.
4. Add pureed tomatoes to the milk mixture. Season and serve at once.

Traditional accompaniment: 2 crackers are crushed into each bowl of soup.

Servings: 4

CORN CHOWDER
   John Young, the Secretary of the Provincial Agricultural Board, authored 38 *Letters of Agricola* which were published in Halifax in 1822. He stated:

> The corns, which Nature has obviously designed as the chief food of man and beast, require no great skill of management; and are withal plants of firm and robust constitution. (p. 65)

This simple to make family favourite provides a savory lunch or a pleasant prelude to a winter dinner. In addition to other nutrients, corn is a good source of protein and the milk supplies all age groups with needed calcium.

3	slices bacon, chopped	3
1	medium onion, chopped	1
3 cups	peeled, sliced potatoes	750mL
1 can	cream style corn	540mL
2 cups	boiling water	500mL
1 teaspoon	salt	5mL
1/2 teaspoon	celery salt	2mL
1/2 teaspoon	pepper	2mL
1 can	evaporated milk	385mL
	or	
1 3/4 cups	whole milk	425mL

1. Fry bacon in saucepan until crisp. Remove and save for garnish.
2. Add onion to fat and saute until transparent.
3. Add boiling water and potatoes. Cook, covered, until potatoes are almost tender.
4. Add corn and seasonings. Bring to just below boiling point.
5. Add milk. Stir until well blended and heated throughout. Ladle into heated soup bowls.

Garnish: crumbled bacon and snipped fresh chives
Servings: 4

PEA SOUP

This soup was originally made with whole yellow or green peas which have to be soaked overnight. The split yellow and green peas can be cooked immediately without pre-soaking.

2 cups	split peas	500mL
2 stalks	celery, diced	2
1 cup	celery leaves, chopped	250mL
3	onions, diced	3
8 cups	cold water	2L
1 tablespoon	salt	15mL
1/2 teaspoon	pepper	2mL
1 cup	peeled, sliced potato	250mL
1 teaspoon	summer savoury	5mL
	ham bone	

1. Pick over the peas. Place in a large pot. Add all ingredients except the potatoes. Cover, bring to the boil and simmer for 2 hours or until the peas are tender.
2. Add potatoes and cook until tender (about 12 minutes). Remove ham bone and puree soup by forcing through a sieve or use a food processor.
3. Reheat and taste for seasoning. Serve garnished with croutons.

Yield: 8 servings

CARROT SOUP

3 cups	carrots	750mL
1	large onion	1
1	large potato	1
1/4 cup	butter	50mL
1/2 teaspoon	thyme	2mL
4 cups	chicken or turkey stock	1L
1/4 cup	cereal cream	50mL
	salt and pepper	
	chopped parsley	

1. Peel and thinly slice carrots and potato; mince onion.
2. Melt butter in large heavy saucepan. Add vegetables, cover and cook over moderately low heat for 10 minutes.
3. Stir in stock, add seasonings, bring to a boil, cover and simmer for 25 minutes.

4. Puree soup by forcing through a large sieve or use a food processor. Return to saucepan. Add cream and reheat. Do not boil. **Serve garnished with chopped parsley.**

Yield: 4 servings

CREAM OF PUMPKIN SOUP

A similiar recipe in an early cookbook was called "Squash and Goose Bone Soup".

3 cups	pumpkin	750mL
1/2	small onion, chopped	1/2
1/4 teaspoon	mace	1mL
1 teaspoon	curry	5mL
2 cups	chicken broth	500mL
1 cup	milk	250mL
1 cup	cereal cream	250mL
2 tablespoons	butter	30mL
	salt, pepper, and nutmeg	

1. Cut the pumpkin in quarters, remove the seeds and stringy pulp. Peel, cut in small pieces, and place with onion, spices and broth in a heavy saucepan. Simmer until pumpkin is very tender.
2. Drain and save broth. Mash or puree pumpkin until it is very smooth.
3. Return pumpkin and liquid to stove. When well heated add the milk, cream, and melted butter. Reheat but do not boil. Season with salt, pepper and sprinkle lightly with freshly ground nutmeg.

Servings: 5

SCOTCH BROTH

William Sloan, whose business was located on Prince William Street **in St. John, offered for sale "Barley in kegs" and "Best Mutton Hams".** The bones of the latter would also be a good base for this **favourite.**

2 quarts	water	2L
1 1/2 **pounds**	lamb bones	.75kg
1/2 cup	medium pearl barley	125mL
	celery leaves	
2 teaspoons	salt	10mL
1	well washed chopped leek	1

34

3	carrots, diced	
1	small turnip, diced	
3	stalks celery, diced	
1	minced onion	
	pepper	
1/2 cup	fresh parsley, minced	125mL

1. In a kettle cover the bones with the water and bring to a boil. Reduce heat and skim froth as it rises to the top.
2. Add barley, celery leaves and salt. Simmer covered for 1 hour.
3. Add leek, carrots, turnip, celery, and onion. Simmer for 30 minutes. Test for seasoning. Remove bones and celery leaves with slotted spoon.
4. Add parsley and serve in heated bowls.

Yield: 10 to 12 servings

NOODLES

A grandmother of a student demonstrated to my high school class the art of preparing and cutting her delectable noodles. The ingredients and method are the same as those found in a sixteenth century cookbook. We served some of the dried noodles with a Chicken Vegetable Soup and the remainder were reheated and served with butter and grated cheddar cheese.

2 cups	flour	500mL
2	eggs	2
1/2 teaspoon	salt	2mL
1/4 cup	water	50mL

1. Sift the flour and salt into a bowl. Beat the eggs and add to the flour along with the water. Using one hand, draw the flour to the center and work it in with the fingers, until the dough is smooth. Place on a lightly floured surface and knead for about 5 minutes or until the dough is very smooth and elastic.
2. Cut the dough into 4 pieces. Set 3 aside and roll the remaining one until it is paper thin. To speed the drying process drape a tea towel over a partially open oven door (temperature turned to warm). Place the thin dough on the towel and leave until slightly dry but still pliable.
3. Repeat the rolling and drying steps with the remaining dough. Fold the dried piece into a 2 inch (5cm) wide rectangle. Place your fingers on the top of the rolled dough, as a guide for thickness of the noodle, and slice through.

4. Spread the cut noodles out on a tablecloth and leave until completely dry (at least 3 hours). Store in sealed plastic bags or covered jars in a dry place.

CROUTONS FOR SOUP

Cut buttered or unbuttered bread in strips. Then cut the bread in the opposite direction to form cubes. Put on a baking sheet and toast in a slow oven 300°F (150°C) until the cubes are golden brown on all sides. Turn occasionally.

VARIATION: CHEESE CROUTONS Sprinkle 1/2 cup (125mL) of grated parmesan cheese on the bread cubes before placing them on the baking sheet.

37

BREADS

JS '83

John D. Smith '82

The settler's favourite yeast for bread making was made at home from hops. Once planted the hardy perennial hop vine grew "luxuriantly" over stone walls, verandahs and outhouses. The yellow blossoms were gathered in August and dried for later use.

Col. Robert Morse, who toured and reported on "the province of Nova Scotia" in the autumn of 1783 and the summer of 1784, mentions the growth of "very fine hops" in the St. John River Valley settlements.

(*Report Canadian Archives,* 1884, Morse's Report, p. xxxviii)

Most recipes for yeast required a "starter". The following "tested" one produced an inexpensive yeast without a starter. Dried hops were obtained from a natural food store. Two weeks after the fermented yeast was bottled, a small portion was used to make Down East Brown Bread.

BREADS

HOME MADE YEAST

1/4 cup hops
2 quarts water
1 tablespoon salt
1 cup sugar
2 cups flour
3 cups cooked mashed potatoes

Boil hops and water for 30 minutes. Let cool to lukewarm. Put in bowl and add salt and sugar. Beat in flour using a whisk. Let stand at room temperature, covered with a cloth for 2 days.

Add mashed potatoes. Let stand 1 day.

Strain mixture through a seive.

Bottle and store in a cool place until ready for use.

Keeps for 2 months.
Yield: 2 quarts

BUCKWHEAT GRIDDLECAKES

Here is a Sunday morning treat which is well worth the effort of a few minutes of pre-preparation on Saturday night. When you eat these, think of Loyalist Alexander Huston who made this entry in his journal on Thurs. Oct. 18 (1787):

> A cold frosty morning. Wind at W. I was digging (potatoes) all day. Capn. Carson was over wanting fire wood. No news in Town. I did take 2 Bushels Buckwheat to the mill.

3/4 teaspoon	dry yeast	3mL
1/4 cup	lukewarm water	50mL
dash	sugar	dash
3/4 cup	buckwheat flour	175mL
3/4 cup	all purpose flour	175mL
1 cup	buttermilk	250mL
1/2 teaspoon	salt	2mL
1	egg	1
1 tablespoon	molasses	15mL

41

| 1/2 teaspoon | baking soda | 2mL |
| 1-2 tablespoons | buttermilk | 15-30mL |

1. Mix sugar with lukewarm water in a large bowl. Add yeast and let stand for 10 minutes.
2. Stir in buckwheat and all purpose flour. Add buttermilk and salt. Beat batter until smooth. Cover with a tea towel and leave on counter overnight. The next morning, stir batter.
3. Beat in egg, molasses and baking soda. Let stand 5 minutes. Add buttermilk if batter is too thick.
4. Heat griddle and brush with oil. Drop batter on the griddle in 3-inch rounds. When top is bubbly and underside is golden, turn the pancake. When the other side is golden transfer to heated platter.
5. Serve hot with butter and maple syrup.

Yield: 3-4 servings.

VELVET WAFFLES

Loyalist cooks used a long-handled wafer or waffle iron. The closed iron was heated in the hot coals for a few minutes and then the hinged end was placed on a thick wooden board. The heated iron was opened, a small amount of dough was placed inside and then the iron was quickly closed while the waffle cooked.

2 cups	all purpose flour	500mL
2 tablespoons	sugar	30mL
1 tablespoon	baking powder	15mL
3/4 teaspoon	salt	3mL
3	well beaten eggs	3
1 3/4 cups	milk	425mL
1/2 cup	vegetable oil	125mL

1. Sift dry ingredients into a bowl.
2. Combine beaten eggs, milk and oil; add to dry ingredients. Beat until smooth. Use about 1/2 cup batter (125mL) for each waffle.
3. Bake in a hot waffle iron until golden brown.

Makes 8 waffles.

MOCK MAPLE SYRUP

1 cup	white sugar	250mL
1 cup	brown sugar	250mL
1 cup	water	250mL
few drops	maple flavouring	f.d.

1. Mix sugars and water in a saucepan. Boil for 5 minutes. Remove from heat. Add maple flavouring. Serve on pancakes, waffles, or ice cream.

SOUR CREAM PANCAKES WITH VARIATIONS

The light texture and pleasing flavour of these pancakes is due to the use of sour cream and to the extra beating during the preparation. When fresh blueberries are in season add them, with a minimum of stirring, just before pouring the mixture on the griddle. Fresh apples can be substituted for added nutrients and a flavour change.

2	well beaten eggs	2
1/4 cup	sugar	50mL
dash	salt	dash
1 cup	flour	250mL
1 teaspoon	baking powder	5mL
1 teaspoon	baking soda	5mL
3/4 cup	sour cream	175mL

1. Beat eggs well. Slowly add sugar beating continuously.
2. Sift flour, baking powder, baking soda and salt. Stir into the egg mixture and then beat well.
3. Add sour cream. Beat and Beat!
4. Drop on heated griddle which has been brushed with oil. When pancake is bubbly on top and golden underneath turn over. Cook until other side is golden, however, since these pancakes are thick make sure centre is cooked. Place on heated platter in a warm oven until all are prepared. Serve with molasses or maple syrup.

Yield: 3-4 servings

BLUEBERRY PANCAKES

Make sour cream pancakes. Carefully fold 1 cup (250mL) of fresh blueberries into the batter, being careful not to crush berries. Cook as above.

APPLE PANCAKES

Make sour cream pancakes. Add 2 large, tart, peeled, quartered, and thinly sliced apples. Fold into the batter before cooking. Serve with cinnamon sugar.

CLOUD BISCUITS

A description of the preparation for a wedding feast held in Shelburne in 1807, included the making of "8 pounds of Drape Biskat". Light, layered tea biscuits are a perennial favourite of all age groups. Teen-age chefs enjoy making the rolled cinnamon variation, while the drop biscuits make a great topping for chicken or tuna pot pies.

2 cups	all purpose flour	500mL
1 tablespoon	sugar	15mL
4 teaspoons	baking powder	20mL
1/2 teaspoon	salt	2mL
1/2 cup	shortening	125mL
1	egg, beaten	1
2/3 cup	milk	150mL

1. Sift together dry ingredients, cut in shortening until mixture resembles coarse crumbs.
2. Combine beaten egg and milk; add to flour mixture all at once. Stir till dough follows fork around the bowl.
3. Knead gently with heel of hand about 20 times. Roll 3/4 inch (2cm) thick. Cut straight down with cutter — do not twist. Place on baking sheet and chill 1-3 hours.
4. Bake in hot 450°F (230°C) for 10-12 minutes.

Yield: 18 biscuits.

CINNAMON PINWHEELS or ROLLMEUPS

Proceed as above. Roll dough into a rectangle. Spread with softened butter. Sprinkle with a mixture of brown sugar and cinnamon. Roll up lengthwise and cut into 12 pieces. Place cut side down on baking sheet. Bake at 375°F (190°C) for 12-15 minutes.

DROP BISCUITS

Increase milk to 1 cup (250mL). Do not knead but drop biscuits from a spoon onto stew or pies and bake uncovered for 25 minutes.

CHEESE BISCUITS

Roll out biscuit dough and sprinkle with 1/2 cup (125mL) of grated cheddar cheese. Roll up like a jelly roll and cut into 1 inch (2.5cm) pieces. Brush with milk. Bake in 400°F (200°C) oven for 10-12 minutes.

44

BANNOCK

A native Indian student prepared bannock for my class, using the recipe and method of preparation which has been handed down from generation to generation in his family.

2 cups	all purpose flour	500mL
1 teaspoon	baking powder	5mL
1/2 teaspoon	salt	2mL
2 tablespoons	sugar	30mL
6 tablespoons	shortening	90mL
1 cup	raisins	250mL
1/2 cup	milk	125mL
1	egg, slightly beaten	1

1. Sift flour, baking powder, sugar and salt together. Add raisins and mix well.
2. Blend egg and milk together and mix into the flour mixture. Add shortening and knead for 3 to 5 minutes. Make into round flat dough and design with fork patterns.
3. Grease baking sheet, and put into 400°F (200°C) oven for about 30 minutes.

CARROT WALNUT MUFFINS

2 cups	flour	500mL
1/4 cup	sugar	50mL
1 tablespoon	baking powder	15mL
1 teaspoon	cinnamon	5mL
1/2 teaspoon	salt	2mL
1/2 cup	grated raw carrot	125mL
1/2 cup	chopped walnuts	125mL
1	egg	1
1 cup	milk	250mL
1/4 cup	oil	50mL

1. Sift dry ingredients together into a large bowl. Mix in carrot and walnuts.
2. Mix liquid ingredients in another bowl. Stir the wet ingredients into the flour mixture until just combined.
3. **Put batter into 12 well greased muffin tins. Bake at 425°F (210°C) for about 20 minutes or until they test done.**

CORN PONES

Indian meal (corn meal) was a staple of the Loyalists. Hot corn breads went by various names such as johnny cakes, ash cakes, hoe cakes and corn pones. If you are an outdoor buff eliminate the baking powder in the following recipe and bake the cakes on a greased hoe before an open fire. They are delicious when served hot and liberally spread with butter and honey or maple syrup. They can be reheated by steaming.

1 1/4 cups	flour	300mL
1/2 teaspoon	salt	2mL
2 tablespoons	sugar	30mL
1 tablespoon	baking powder	15mL
3/4 cup	corn meal	175mL
1	egg	1
1 cup	milk	250mL
2 tablespoons	melted shortening	30mL

1. Sift the flour, baking powder, sugar and salt into a bowl. Stir in the corn meal and combine thoroughly.
2. Beat the egg, add the milk and shortening. Add liquid ingredients to the dry mixture stirring only enough to combine ingredients.
3. Spoon into well greased corn pone pans or greased muffin tins. Bake at 400°F (200°C) for about 15 minutes.

Yield: 12 pones

CORN FLOUR SCONES

These have a lighter texture than corn pones and are a great accompaniment for home made soup.

1 1/2 cups	all purpose flour	375mL
1/2 cup	corn flour	125mL
2 tablespoons	sugar	30mL
1 tablespoon	baking powder	15mL
1/2 teaspoon	salt	2mL
1/2 cup	butter	125mL
2/3 cup	buttermilk	150mL

1. Sift dry ingredients into a bowl. Cut in butter, using a pastry blender, until mixture resembles coarse crumbs.

46

2. Stir in buttermilk. Form dough into a ball. Roll dough into 3/4 inch (2cm) thick circle and with a 2 1/2 inch (4cm) cutter cut out rounds.
3. Place on a baking sheet in a 400⁰F (200⁰C) oven for approximately 20 minutes. Split and serve hot with butter.

Yield: 10 scones

SQUASH MUFFINS

Save enough squash the next time you bake it to treat the family later with these muffins. They are rich in flavour, vitamin A and iron.

3/4 cup	brown sugar	175mL
1/4 cup	molasses	50mL
1/2 cup	butter	125mL
1	beaten egg	1
1 cup	cooked, mashed squash	250mL
1 3/4 cup	flour	425mL
1 teaspoon	baking soda	5mL
1/4 teaspoon	salt	1mL

1. Prepare squash. Cream butter and sugar. Add molasses, beaten egg and squash. Blend well.
2. Sift flour, baking soda and salt; stir into squash mixture. Fill well greased muffin tins. Bake at 375⁰F. (190⁰C.) about 25 minutes.

Yield: 12 large muffins

BLUEBERRY MUFFINS

Fresh blueberry muffins are one of the joys of a Maritime summer. This recipe is so rich you can serve them without butter.

1/4 cup	butter	50mL
1/4 cup	sugar	50mL
1	egg, well beaten	1
2 cups	flour	500mL
4 teaspoons	baking powder	20mL
1/2 teaspoon	salt	2mL
1 cup	milk	250mL
2 cups	fresh blueberries or dry pack frozen	500mL

47

1. Cream butter, add sugar and egg. Mix well.
2. Sift flour with baking powder and salt. Add to first mixture alternately with milk. Mix well. Fold in blueberries. Do *not* beat.
3. Fill greased muffin pans. Bake in 375°F (190°C) oven about 25 minutes.

Yield: 12 large muffins

SCOTCH SCONES

3 cups	all purpose flour	750mL
1 teaspoon	cream of tartar	5mL
1/2 teaspoon	baking soda	2mL
1 teaspoon	salt	5mL
1 cup	lard	250mL
1/2 cup	white sugar	125mL
1	egg, beaten	1
1/2 cup	milk	125mL
1/2 cup	raisins	125mL

1. Sift flour, cream of tartar, baking soda and salt into a bowl. Cut in the lard with a pastry blender.
2. Add sugar, beaten egg and milk. Mix with a fork and then stir in raisins.
3. Roll dough into a 1/2 inch (1.5cm) thick circle. Cut in triangles. Place on baking sheet and bake in 350°F (180°C) oven for about 20 minutes.

Yield: 12 scones

SPICED CURRANT MUFFINS

Wild black and red currants were picked in the summer and dried for later use. They were also advertised for sale by the local merchants in 150 pound to 200 pound weight casks!

1 1/2 cups	currants	375mL
2 cups	water	500mL
1/4 cup	butter	50mL
3/4 cup	sugar	175mL
1	egg, beaten	1
1 teaspoon	vanilla	5mL
1 1/2 cups	flour	375mL

1 teaspoon	baking soda	5mL
1 teaspoon	cinnamon	5mL
1 teaspoon	cloves	5mL
1/4 teaspoon	salt	1mL

1. Put currants and water in a saucepan and boil uncovered for 20 minutes. (Should have 3/4 cup (175mL) of liquid). Cool.
2. Cream butter and sugar in a bowl. Add egg and vanilla. Mix well. Add sifted dry ingredients. Add cooled currants and liquid and stir only to moisten.
3. Put in greased muffin tins. Bake at 375°F (190°C) for 25 minutes.

Yield: 12 muffins

CINNAMON APPLE MUFFINS

...About ten days ago, I had a present of well toward a bushel of as fine, fair, sound, high flavoured apples as you ever saw at New York in the month of January.
General Timothy Ruggles to Edward Winslow Sr.
Annapolis, 17 July, 1783.[1]

The surprise fresh flavour of apple in these muffins provides a treat at any season of the year.

2 cups	flour	500mL
1/2 cup	sugar	125mL
4 teaspoons	baking powder	20mL
1/2 teaspoon	salt	2mL
1 teaspoon	cinnamon	5mL
1	egg	1
1 cup	milk (scant)	225ml
4 tablespoons	butter, melted	50mL
1 cup	diced apples	250mL

1. Measure and sift dry ingredients into a bowl. Make a well in the centre.
2. Combine milk, beaten egg, and melted butter and pour into the well. Mix only until combined. Fold in apples.
3. Fill 12 well greased muffin tins. Sprinkle tops with a mixture of cinnamon and sugar. Bake at 425°F (210°C) for 15 minutes or until done.

RICH BRAN MUFFINS

Buttermilk, a by-product of making butter was always available and well utilized by the early settlers.

1 1/2 cups	natural bran	375mL
1 cup	buttermilk	250mL
2 tablespoons	melted shortening	30mL
1/4 cup	table molasses	50mL
1	egg	1
1/2 teaspoon	salt	2mL
1 cup	flour	250mL
1/2 teaspoon	baking powder	2mL
1/2 teaspoon	baking soda	2mL

1. Mix bran and buttermilk in a bowl and let stand for 10 minutes.
2. Beat egg. Add the melted shortening, molasses and salt. Beat until light.
3. Sift flour, baking powder and baking soda into the bran mixture. Stir in the egg mixture and mix only enough to combine ingredients.
4. Fill 12 well greased muffin tins and bake at 375ºF (190ºC) for 20 minutes or until done.

CRANBERRY ORANGE MUFFINS

Cranberries, an indigenous crop, were served in many ways. Seafaring vessels often carried quantities of cranberries floating in wooden flasks filled with cold water which provided both a supply of fresh water and a food source to prevent scurvy.

3/4 cup	cranberry halves	175mL
1/3 cup	sugar	75mL
2 cups	flour	500mL
1 tablespoon	baking powder	15mL
1/2 teaspoon	salt	2mL
2 tablespoons	sugar	30mL
1	egg, beaten	1
1 cup	milk	250mL
4 tablespoons	melted shortening	60mL
1 teaspoon	grated orange rind	5mL

1. Mix cranberry halves with the sugar and let stand while preparing muffin mixture.

50

2. Sift dry ingredients into a bowl. Add egg, milk, shortening, orange rind and sugared cranberries. Mix but do not beat.
3. Put in 12 well greased muffin tins and bake at 350°F (180°C) for about 20 minutes.

In Special Sessions
1795 – 35ᵗʰ Geo. 3.

Monday January 12ᵗʰ

Court open'd by Proclamation

The Court upon the representation of the Bakers having caused an inquiry, for to be made of the Price of Flour are informed that good Inspected Flour can be purchased in this Town for Seven Dollars per Barrel. Whereupon it is Ordered that from and after the 13ᵗʰ Instant the Six penny Loaf made of good sound Wheaten Flour shall weigh 2 lbᵗ 6 oᵤ. avoirdupois weight and smaller Loaves in proportions. This assize to continue till further orders

Facsimilie (by Andrea Smith) of p. 338 *Shelburne County Sessions Court Records, Monday January 12, 1795.*

The Court of Special Sessions frequently heard representations from either the citizens of the town or the bakers regarding the price of bread. As soon as the price of flour was reduced the citizens would request a decrease in the price of bread and vice versa. If the request was granted a new Assize of Bread would be posted and printed in the papers.

A barrel of flour weighed 196 pounds.

Flour was often scarce in all the Loyalist settlements, and the settlers learned to stretch or supplement the flour by using buckwheat, cornmeal, and oatmeal. The recipes for Oatmeal Raisin and Buckwheat Bread use combined grains and yield truly delicious and very nutritious breads. The Steamed Brown Bread which always accompanied the Saturday night baked beans, (and still does) is made with three types of flour.

OATMEAL RAISIN BREAD (a quick bread)

1 cup	rolled oats	250mL
1 cup	buttermilk	250mL
1/2 cup	dark brown sugar	125mL
1	egg, well beaten	1
1 cup	whole wheat flour	250mL
1 teaspoon	baking powder	5mL
1 teaspoon	salt	5mL
1/2 teaspoon	baking soda	2mL
6 tablespoons	melted butter	90mL
1/2 cup	raisins	125mL

1. Soak rolled oats in buttermilk for one hour or longer.
2. Stir in beaten egg and brown sugar. Sift flour, baking powder, salt, and baking soda into the oats mixture. Combine well.
3. Stir in the cooled butter and raisins. Pour into a well greased 8x4x3 (2L) loaf pan. Bake at 400°F (200°C) for 40 minutes or until done.

BUCKWHEAT BREAD (a yeast bread)

1 cup	milk, scalded	250mL
1 cup	boiling water	250mL
2 tablespoons	butter	30mL
1 tablespoon	honey	15mL
1 tablespoon	salt	15mL
1 tablespoon	dry yeast	15mL
1/4 cup	lukewarm water	50mL
1 cup	buckwheat flour	250mL
1 cup	whole wheat flour	250mL
3 1/2-4 cups	all purpose flour	1L

1. Put scalded milk, boiling water, butter, honey and salt in a large bowl and let cool to lukewarm.
2. Dissolve a pinch of sugar in the lukewarm water, add the yeast and let stand for 10 minutes.
3. Stir buckwheat and whole wheat flours into the lukewarm milk mixture. Add yeast mixture. Combine well. Work in 1 1/2 cups (375mL) of white flour to make a dough. Transfer to a lightly floured surface and knead in enough flour to make a smooth soft dough which does not stick to the surface.
4. Knead for 5 minutes. Place dough in a greased bowl turning the dough until it is buttered on all sides. Cover with a clean cloth and leave in a warm place to rise until doubled (about 1 hour).
5. Punch down dough, divide in half and shape into 2 loaves. Place in greased 2L loaf tins and let rise until doubled. (Cover while rising). Bake at 375ºF (190ºC) for about 30 minutes or until done. Turn onto a rack to cool.

Yield: 2 loaves

STEAMED BROWN BREAD

This is a must when you serve home baked beans:

1 cup	sour milk* or buttermilk	250mL
1/2 cup	molasses	125mL
1/2 cup	whole wheat flour	125mL
1/2 cup	cornmeal	125mL
1/2 cup	white flour	125mL
1 teaspoon	baking soda	5mL
1/2 teaspoon	salt	2mL

1. Mix dry ingredients. Add molasses and milk.
2. Put in the top of a greased double boiler and steam 2 1/2 hours. Serve hot, cut in wedges and buttered. Freezes well and can be reheated.

*To sour milk: Combine 1 tablespoon (15mL) of lemon juice or vinegar with 1 cup (250mL) milk. Let stand 5 minutes before using.

DOWN EAST BROWN BREAD

2 cups	rolled oats	500mL
1 cup	cornmeal	250mL
1 1/2 teaspoons	baking soda	7mL
1 tablespoon	salt	15mL
4 tablespoons	shortening	60mL
1/2 cup	brown sugar	125mL
5 cups	boiling water	1.25L
1 cup	lukewarm water	250mL
2 tablespoons	active dry yeast	30mL
1 cup	molasses, table	250mL
1 cup	**whole wheat flour**	250mL
10-11 cups	white flour	2.5-2.75L

1. Mix oats, cornmeal, baking soda, shortening, salt and brown sugar in a large bowl. Pour over the boiling water. Stir and let cool.
2. Dissolve 1 teaspoon sugar in the lukewarm water. Add the yeast. Let stand for 10 minutes.
3. Meanwhile add molasses and whole wheat flour to the oats mixture. Let cool to lukewarm.
4. Add the dissolved yeast to the lukewarm oats. Mix well. Add 3 cups (750mL) white flour. Beat well.
5. Work in 7-8 cups (2L) of white flour with a rotating motion of the hand. Knead on lightly floured surface from 8-10 minutes.
6. Shape into a ball. Put dough in a greased bowl rotating to grease the surface. Cover and let rise in a warm place until doubled in bulk (about 1 1/2 hours). Punch down dough and shape into loaves and rolls.
7. Cover and let rise again until doubled (about 1 hour). Bake in 375°F (190°C) for 30 to 45 minutes.

Yield: 2 loaves and 18 rolls.

SHELBURNE, *June 28*, 1786.

Aſſize of Bread;

As this day ordered by the Court of *Special Seſſions.*

Firſt quality.	lb.	oz.
Six-penny loaf to weigh	2	9
Three-penny ditto,	1	4½
Three half-penny ditto,		10¼

Second qualiſy.	lb.	
Six penny loaf to weigh	3	
Three-penny ditto,	1½	
Three half-penny ditto,	¾	

Rye Flour and *Rye and Indian Meal.*

	lb.
Six-penny loaf to-weigh	4
Three-penny ditto,	2
Three half-penny ditto,	1

JO۱N MILLER *Clerk of Market.*

Nova Scotia Packet Nov. 2, 1786.

Another decision of the Court of Special Sessions on Wednesday June 28, 1786 was:

> ...That a proper person be appointed to Visit the different Bak Houses and all other places where Bread is sold at least three times in every week with directions to examine the Quality as well as the Weight of the different Kinds of Bread and to seize all that may Not be made according to these regulations. p. 61.

July 27, 1786 *Nova Scotia Packet* carried an additional regulation:

> Every Baker is by Act required to Mark his bread with the letter of his Christian and Sir Name under penalty of having it seized and forfeited to the Poor of the town.

55

AUNT MABEL'S PRIZE WHITE BREAD

The flavour and texture of this bread is irresistible — make it and you'll agree it would still rate first in a national contest.

1/2 cup	lukewarm water	125mL
1 teaspoon	sugar	5mL
1 package	dry yeast	1
3 1/2 cups	warm milk	875mL
2 tablespoons	sugar	30mL
1 tablespoon	salt	15mL
2 tablespoons	butter	30mL
9 cups (approximately)	flour	2.25L

1. Dissolve sugar in the lukewarm water and add yeast. Let stand 10 minutes.
2. Combine warm milk, sugar, salt and butter in a large bowl. Beat in 4 cups (1L) of flour. Add the dissolved yeast. Work in about 5 more cups (1.25L) of flour. Place on a lightly floured surface and knead 8 to 10 minutes. Shape into a ball.
3. Place in a greased bowl rotate the dough so the top is greased. Cover and let rise until doubled in bulk (1-1 1/2 hours).
4. Punch down dough and shape into rolls and loaves. Place these in greased pans, cover, and let rise until doubled. Bake at 375°F (190°C) for 35-40 minutes. **Remove from pans and cool on racks.**

Yield: 18 rolls and 2 loaves

RYE AND INDIAN MEAL BREAD

A nutritious and tasty bread which keeps well. It was the cheapest bread available from the bakeries in the early years of the Loyalist settlements.

2 tablespoons	dry yeast	30mL
2 teaspoons	sugar	10mL
1 cup	lukewarm water	250mL
1/4 cup	shortening	50mL
2 teaspoons	salt	10mL
1/3 cup	molasses	75mL
2 cups	buttermilk, warmed	500mL
1 cup	whole wheat flour	250mL
2 cups	rye flour	500mL

| 1/2 cup | corn meal | 125mL |
| 3 1/2 cups | white flour | 875mL |

1. Dissolve sugar in the lukewarm water and add yeast. Let stand 10 minutes.
2. Beat together the shortening, salt and molasses. Add the warmed buttermilk and whole wheat flour. Beat well. Add the rye flour and beat again.
3. Stir in the yeast and then add the cornmeal and part of the white flour. Work the remaining flour in with the hands until a smooth dough. Turn out on floured board and knead for 10 minutes.
4. Place in greased bowl rotating dough so the top will be greased. Cover and let rise in a warm place until doubled in bulk (about 1 1/2 hours). Punch dough, shape into 2 loaves and place in greased pans. Cover and let rise until doubled.
5. Bake at 375°F (190°C) for 45 minutes.

Yield: 2 loaves

Exportation of Grain — We have again the pleasure to inform the Public that a quantity of Grain was last week exported from this town to Fanningsborough, in Nova Scotia. — Can the fruitfulness and superiority of the soil of this country be manifested in a more incontrovertible manner, asks a Correspondent?
Royal Gazette and Miscellany of the Island of St. John, July 29, 1791.

ANADAMA or YANKEE BREAD

This very tasty brown and crusty bread with a chewy, springy texture has an interesting folk tale about its origin. Anna was a lazy housewife. Her husband, exasperated with always coming home to a cold mush, grabbed some yeast, flour and molasses and kneaded it into a dough muttering "Anna, damm her". The result was Anadama Bread:

1 1/2 cups	boiling water	375mL
1 teaspoon	salt	5mL
1/3 cup	yellow corn meal	75mL
1/4 cup	molasses	50mL
1 1/2 tablespoons	butter	20mL
1 package	dry yeast	1
1/4 cup	lukewarm water	50mL

3 3/4 to 4 cups	flour	900mL
2 tablespoons	melted butter	25mL
1 tablespoon	cornmeal	15mL

1. Pour the boiling water over the salt and the cornmeal in a saucepan. Bring to the boiling point and immediately remove from the heat. Stir.
2. Add molasses and butter. Stir. Place in a large bowl and cool to lukewarm. Dissolve yeast in lukewarm water. Let stand 10 minutes, and then add to lukewarm cornmeal mixture.
3. Add flour, gradually kneading in the last cup. Place on a floured board and knead for 10 minutes as it takes time to work in the flour. Dough remains sticky.
4. Place dough in a greased bowl, cover, and let rise until doubled in bulk (1 1/2 hours). Press down dough.
5. Place on board, flatten with hands until dough is the length of the pan and twice as wide. Fold from both sides to the middle. Place in a well greased loaf pan with the seam side down. Let rise until double in bulk (about 1 hour).
6. Brush loaf with melted butter and sprinkle corn meal on top. Bake at 350°F (180°C) for 40-45 minutes. Turn on rack to cool.

Yield: 1 large loaf

HOT CROSS BUNS

2 cups	milk	500 mL
4 tablespoons	butter	60mL
2/3 cup	sugar	150mL
2 teaspoons	cinnamon	10mL
1/2 teaspoon	nutmeg	2mL
2 teaspoons	salt	10mL
1 package	dry yeast	1
1/2 cup	lukewarm water	125mL
3	eggs, well beaten	3
1/2 cup	raisins	125mL
1/2 cup	currants	125mL
6-7 cups	flour	1.5L
2 tablespoons	molasses	30mL
2 tablespoons	milk	30mL

1. Heat milk to scalding point and pour over sugar, cinnamon, nutmeg, salt and butter. Stir until the butter is dissolved. Cool to lukewarm.

58

2. Dissolve 1 teaspoon sugar in the lukewarm water. Sprinkle yeast over and let stand 10 minutes.
3. Mix 1 cup (250mL) of the flour with the raisins and currants. Add to the milk mixture. When cool add the beaten eggs and the yeast.
4. Beat in 2 cups (500mL) of the flour. Beat vigourously. Work in the remaining flour with a rotating motion of the hand. The dough should remain slightly moist.
5. Place in a greased bowl. Cover and let rise until doubled. Shape into buns. Place one inch apart in greased pans and let rise again.
6. Bake in 400°F (200°C) oven 20 to 30 minutes. When done remove from the oven and brush with the molasses milk mixture. When cool make the shape of a cross on each bun with icing sugar mixed with cream.

Yield: 30 buns

Cheap, Cheap.

Now Selling in Charlotte Town,
FOR CASH ONLY,
Excellent New York Flour & Bread,
lower than ever yet sold in this Island,
... viz.
Superfine Flour, at 7 Dollars per Barrel.
Fine   do.   6 do.   do.
Middlings   4 ½   do.
Fine Bread, at 5 Dollars per Barrel.
Ship Do. at 3½ Dollars per Do.
An Allowance will be made to those who
will purchase the whole. Apply to Mr.
James Frazer.

Royal Gazette and Miscellany of the Island of St. John. July 14, 1792.

PUMPKIN BREAD

This delicious bread is an excellent source of vitamin A, is rich in iron, and freezes beautifully. It can be served plain, buttered, or spread with cream cheese.

1 can	pumpkin	540mL
	or	
2 cups	cooked pumpkin	500mL
2 cups	white sugar	500mL
1/2 cup	oil	125mL
4	eggs	4
3 cups	flour	750mL
4 teaspoons	cinnamon	20mL
2 teaspoons	salt	10mL
2 teaspoons	soda	10mL
2 teaspoons	baking powder	10mL
1 1/2 cups	raisins	375mL

1. Mix oil and sugar. Add eggs beating well after each addition.
2. Add pumpkin and then stir in raisins.
3. Sift dry ingredients together and add. Mix well.
4. Pour into well greased pans. Large empty tins (such as tomato or coffee) make an interesting shaped loaf, or use loaf pan.
5. Bake at 350°F (180°C) for 1 hour or until tester comes out clean.

Yield: 2 loaves

STREUSEL-LAYERED COFFEECAKE

Streusel Mixture

1/2 cup	firmly packed brown sugar	125mL
2 tablespoons	butter	30mL
2 tablespoons	flour	30mL
1 teaspoon	cinnamon	5mL

Batter

1 1/2 cups	flour	375mL
2 1/2 teaspoons	baking powder	12mL
1/2 teaspoon	salt	2mL
1	egg	1
3/4 cup	sugar	175mL
1/3 cup	butter	75mL
1/2 cup	milk	125mL

1 teaspoon	vanilla	5mL

1. Preheat oven to 375ºF (190ºC). Grease one 8x8 (2L) cake pan.
2. Make streusel mixture: In small bowl, combine brown sugar, butter, flour and cinnamon. Mix with fork until crumbly. Set aside.
3. Make batter: Sift flour, baking powder, and salt. Cream butter and sugar in a medium bowl. Add beaten egg and vanilla. Beat until light. Add flour mixture and milk alternately.
4. Place 1/2 of the batter in the pan. Sprinkle with part of streusel crumbs. Repeat.
5. Bake 25 minutes or until cake tests done. Serve warm.

CHEESE WAFERS

> Dr. and Mrs. Walters came to tea last evening gave Bread and cheese afterwards.
> Captain William Booth   April 24, 1789

It was customary to invite a couple of friends (male or female) in for afternoon tea and conversation. Wafers, tarts, and sweetmeats (candied fruits and nuts) were usually served along with the tea. Double Gloucester was the cheese which appeared most frequently in the newspaper advertisements.

1/2 cup	butter	125mL
1/2 cup	shredded cheese (cheddar)	125mL
2 cups	flour	500mL
4-5 tablespoons	water	60-75mL
	paprika	
	melted butter	

1. Use a pastry cutter to mix the butter and cheese into the flour. When the mixture resembles fine crumbs add part of the water. Mix with a fork and add enough water to make a dough which can be formed into a ball.
2. Roll dough into a circle and cut with a 1 inch round cutter.
3. Place rounds on an ungreased baking sheet. Brush with melted butter and sprinkle with paprika. Bake at 450ºF (220ºC) for about 8 minutes.

Yield: 50 wafers

CHEESE PUFFS

1 cup	water	250mL
1/4 cup	butter	50mL
1 cup	flour	250mL
1/4 teaspoon	salt	1mL
3	eggs	3
1/2 cup	grated cheddar cheese	125mL

1. Heat water, butter and salt to a rolling boil in a saucepan. Stir in flour all at once. Stir vigourously over low heat until mixture leaves pan to form a ball.
2. Remove from heat. Add eggs one at a time beating thoroughly after each addition.
3. Fold in grated cheese. Drop by teaspoonfuls on a greased baking sheet, leaving 1 inch between each puff.
4. Bake at 425ºF (210ºC) for 10 minutes. Reduce heat to 375ºF (190ºC) and bake about 10 more minutes. Transfer to a rack and let stand for 10 minutes before serving.

Yield: 36-40 puffs

Ships left the Loyalist port's laden with cargoes of salt fish and lumber. Those which returned from the West Indies carried sugar, molasses, spices, coffee, rum and other spirits and a variety of tropical fruits.

DATE BREAD

1 cup	dates	250mL
1 cup	boiling water	250mL
1	egg	1
dash	salt	dash
1 tablespoon	butter	15mL
1 teaspoon	soda	5mL
1 teaspoon	vanilla	5mL
1 1/2 cups	flour	375mL
3/4 cup	sugar	175mL

1. Pour boiling water over the finely chopped dates and butter. Let cool.
2. When mixture is cool add sugar, salt, soda, vanilla, egg and flour to the date mixture.

3. Put in a greased loaf pan in a 350°F (180°C) oven for almost an hour. This bread can also be baked in round tins. It slices better and improves in flavour if kept for a day before serving.

LEMON BREAD

1/2 cup	shortening	125mL
1 cup	sugar	250mL
2	eggs, beaten	2
1	lemon rind	1
1 teaspoon	baking powder	5mL
dash	salt	dash
1 1/2 cup	flour	375mL
1/2 cup	milk	125mL
	walnuts (optional)	

1. Cream shortening and sugar. Add eggs and lemon rind. Beat until very light.
2. Sift flour, baking powder and salt together. Add flour mixture alternately with the milk (beginning and ending with flour).
3. Put in a greased loaf pan and bake at 350°F (180°C) for about 45 minutes.
4. When loaf tests done remove from the oven. Make a topping of the juice of 1 lemon and 1/4 cup (50mL) of white sugar. Pour over the loaf and let it seep in. Turn loaf out on a rack to cool.

FISH

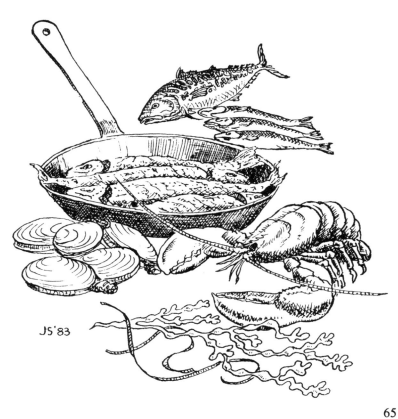

JS'83

Jordan River, N.S.

...in the Spring Gasperaus or alewives come in the Middle of April and run until about the tenth of may in great abundance, and are exported to the west Indies." p. 40.

Reverend James Munroe, 1795.

FISH

ALEWIVES, GASPEREAUX, KIACKS

A fish with three commonly used names still provides springtime fun and food from rivers along the Atlantic seaboard. The Loyalists welcomed the spawning run of "Alewives", the French settlers of "Gaspereaux" and the Micmac Indians of "Kiacks". They are easily caught with dipnets and are often salted and packed in barrels on the spot.

SMOKED KIACK (not tested)

Clean and scale kiacks but leave the heads on. Make a brine of salt and water strong enough to float a raw potato. Put fish in this brine and leave for 48 hours. Hang fish to dry for two days in a cool, shaded place. Cut hackmatack skewers long enough to hang across a barrel which has both the top and bottom removed. String fish by their heads on these skewers. The fish should not touch one another. Use hardwood, with bark removed, to make a good fire and when burning briskly smother with hardwood sawdust. Place the barrel with the attached fish over the smoking embers. Cover the barrel with burlap or canvas to keep the heat and smoke in the barrel. Leave 4 hours.

POACHED SMOKED KIACK (Gaspereaux)

Remove head and tail from the smoked fish. Simmer below the boiling point for 20 minutes. The skin lifts away easily before serving. Season with salt, pepper and lemon juice to taste. These make a delicious appetizer or can be served as a supper dish with potatoes and vegetables.

SLOW POKES OR SOUSED FRESH KIACK

Fillet 6 fresh kiack and remove the backbone. Season with salt and pepper, roll each fillet into a pinwheel and secure with a toothpick. Pack closely into a casserole dish and cover with 1 cup (250mL) vinegar and 1 teaspoon (5mL) of sugar. Bake in 350°F (180°C) oven for 1 1/2 hours. Allow to cool in juices. Serve cold as a salad.

ATLANTIC MACKEREL

...and the men are fishing for mackerel. Mr. Mills has caught the first one. I never saw a live one before. It is the handsomest fish I ever beheld."
On board the *Two Sisters*. June 16, 1783 Sara Frost[1]

When schools of mackerel start to arrive along the Atlantic coast in early June they are a popular catch. Fresh mackerel, with its distinctive, rich flavour is best grilled or baked. The Loyalists greased a gridiron* with butter or salt pork, placed the seasoned mackerel on the iron and broiled it over the coals. Gooseberry or cranberry sauce was served with the mackerel to balance the oiliness of the fish and to enhance the taste. Large quantities of mackerel were salted in barrels or smoked either for export or for use in the winter months. The salt mackerel was freshened by soaking in several changes of fresh water before cooking. Soused mackerel has always been a popular dish. The long slow cooking in a spiced vinegar dissolves the bones which means easy eating and additional calcium in the diet.

*Note the gridiron attached to the mantlepiece in the kitchen hearth drawing page 18.

BROILED MACKEREL

2	fresh, filleted mackerel	2
1/4 cup	melted butter	50mL
1/2 teaspoon	salt	2mL
dash	pepper	dash

1. Wipe mackerel and place on a greased broiling rack. Brush fish with melted butter.
2. Broil 3-4 inches (8-10cm) from heat. When browned on one side, season, turn and broil the other side.
3. Cook until fish is opaque, or approximately 10 minutes. Serve with lemon wedges.

Yield: 4 servings

BAKED MACKEREL

2	whole mackerel (or 4 fillets)	2
3 tablespoons	flour	45mL
2	medium onions	2
2 tablespoons	melted butter	30mL
1-1 1/2 cups	cereal cream or blend salt, pepper, tarragon	250mL

68

1. Wipe mackerel and cut in serving-size pieces. Roll in flour seasoned with salt, pepper and tarragon.
2. Place fish skin side down in a shallow baking pan.
3. Slice onion over the mackerel and dot with butter. Pour in cream to almost cover the fish.
4. Bake uncovered at 375°F. (190°C.) for 30 minutes.
5. Serve with baked potatoes and a tart sauce such as gooseberry, cranberry, or rhubarb.

Yield: 4 servings

SOUSED MACKEREL or HERRING

3-5	cleaned mackerel	3-5
1 teaspoon	salt	5mL
2 tablespoons	pickling spice	30mL
1 cup	vinegar	250mL
1/2 cup	water	125mL
1	chopped onion	1

1. Cut mackerel in serving-size pieces and place in casserole dish, or remove backbone and roll up lengthwise.
2. Tie spices loosely in cheesecloth bag. Place in dish and add vinegar, salt, water and onion. Bake uncovered in 350°F. (180°C.) oven for 2 hours.
3. Serve either hot or cold.

Yield: 6-8 servings

FLOUNDER (SOLE)

Known to most Maritimers as flounder, but marketed as sole, this is a lean finely textured fish with a delicate flavour. It is harvested by both inshore and offshore vessels and would have been regularly available at the Loyalist fish markets.

BROILED FILLET OF SOLE

1 pound	sole fillets	.5kg
1 cup	fine bread crumbs	250mL
1/2 cup	grated cheddar cheese	125mL
2 tablespoons	minced fresh parsley	30mL
1/4 teaspoon	curry powder	1mL
1/2 cup	melted butter	125mL
2 tablespoons	softened butter	30mL
	salt and pepper	

1. Flatten the fillets slightly between two pieces of wax paper. Season with salt and pepper. Place in one layer in a shallow greased broiling pan.
2. Prepare the dressing by mixing the bread crumbs, cheese, parsley, curry powder and melted butter. Sprinkle on top of the sole.
3. Dot the fish with softened butter. Broil three inches from the heat of a preheated broiler for 5-7 minutes. Frozen fillets will take longer. Test for doneness with a fork — the fish should flake easily. Serve with lemon wedges.

Yield: 3 servings

BAKED SOLE or HADDOCK FILLETS

"The Haddock runs in great plenty all summer and are caught for the peoples own use, they do not export them." p. 40.
　　　Reverend Munroe　　1795

1 pound	sole or haddock fillets	.5kg
	juice of lemon	
1/4 cup	melted butter	50mL
	parsley flakes, salt, pepper	

1. Cut fish in serving portions. Place in a single layer in greased baking dish.
2. Pour lemon juice over fish, season with salt and pepper. Add melted butter and minced parsley. Bake at 400⁰F (200⁰C) for 15 minutes or until fish flakes easily with fork.

Yield: 3 servings

GRILLED HALIBUT or SALMON STEAKS or BROOK TROUT

Alexander Huston expressed his delight that spring was coming in his March 15, 1788 diary entry:

"There was fresh fish in the market and wild geese began to fly this day."

The delicate flavour of truly fresh fish responds best to the simplest cooking methods. The Loyalist used a greased gridiron while today's cooks use a broiler rack.

2 pounds	fresh fish	1kg
2 tablespoons	melted butter	30mL
1 tablespoon	lemon juice	15mL

1/4 teaspoon	marjoram	1mL

1. Preheat broiling unit and broiling rack about 10 minutes. Make a basting sauce of butter, lemon juice and marjoram.
2. Measure thickness of the steak, if thinner than 1 inch (3cm) there is a tendency to dry out during broiling so marinate steaks for 30 minutes.
3. Place basted fish on greased broiling rack (trout skin side down). Put pan 3-5 inches (8-13cm) from the heat (depending on the thickness of the fish). When golden brown turn, baste and broil other side. Total cooking time per inch thickness is 10 minutes per inch (4 minutes per cm.).
4. Serve immediately.

BAKED STUFFED HALIBUT OR SALMON

Atlantic Halibut and Atlantic Salmon are both considered delicacies and fetch higher prices than other flatfish. Each is sumptuous when baked stuffed and served with a drawn butter sauce. Either stuff the whole dressed fish or the fillets — the latter way makes serving easier.

6-7 pounds	halibut or salmon	3kg
1/3 cup	onion, chopped	75mL
1/3 cup	celery, diced	75mL
3 tablespoons	butter, melted	45mL
1 teaspoon	salt	5mL
1/2 teaspoon	summer savoury	2mL
1/2 teaspoon	sage	2mL
dash	pepper	dash
3 cups	bread crumbs	750mL
1	medium apple, diced	1

1. Clean and fillet the fish. Butter a sheet of foil large enough to wrap around the salmon. Grease the foil well and place in a shallow baking pan.
2. Place a fillet on the foil and stuff with the prepared bread dressing. To prepare the dressing: melt the butter in a skillet and saute the onion and celery until tender. Add the seasonings, apple and bread crumbs. Either stuff the fish or place stuffing on a fillet. Cover with the second fillet.
3. Fold foil over fish and seal in a packet. Place on prepared pan in 450°F (220°C) oven, allowing 10 minutes per inch thickness (4 minutes per cm thickness).

Yield: 10 servings

71

DRAWN BUTTER SAUCE

Delicious with grilled or baked fish.

1/4 cup	butter	50mL
2 tablespoons	flour	30mL
1/4 teaspoon	salt	1mL
dash	pepper	dash
1 cup	boiling water	250mL
1 tablespoon	lemon juice	15mL

1. Melt one half of the butter, blend in flour and seasonings. Gradually add the boiling water; cook and stir over low heat until thickened.
2. Remove from heat and add remaining butter in pieces. Finally add lemon juice.

Yield: 1 cup

MAITRE D'HOTEL BUTTER

Another delicious accompaniment for baked or grilled fish.

4 tablespoons	butter	50mL
2 tablespoons	minced parsley	30mL
2 tablespoons	lemon juice	30mL
1 teaspoon	salt	5mL
1/4 teaspoon	pepper	2mL

Put butter in a bowl, and whisk with a wooden spoon until creamy. Add salt, pepper, parsley and lemon juice. Mix well. Butter paddles can be used to make into small balls or serve in one piece on a dish.

Shelburn Oct 23, 1789

D. Sire:

I wrote you the first Instant and was then in a hurry I could not find you some of the Staples of this Country I now sende you to the Care of W'm McKee Meritt. in N York a Bbl. Salmon which you may either Smoke or Eat as out the Pickle soaking it 24 hours Keeping a weight on the fish when you open the Barrel and the Glass it will keep to the last fish Good.

It is rather too soon for Apples Cyder Pears and other fruit but the month November should not be neglected and if you can supply me with what is good had rather give you the preference I wish you to send me by first Opportunly few pear trees Sorted 10 plumb Trees sorted Six Quince Trees and some good Slips of Gooseberry and Philberts. I have Bought a farm and wish to improve it.

Your friend and Humble Servt.

S. Skinner

Facsimilie of Stephen Skinner's letter to James Schornorton, South Amboy, New Jersey

SALT COD AND PORK SCRAPS

According to the 1790 Shelburne Court Records the rations provided for the poor were salt fish, salt pork, potatoes, indian meal and molasses. They were also the staples for many Loyalist families.

Today salt cod and pork scraplings is served as a popular speciality dish in taverns and coastal restaurants. Many menus use original pioneer names sugh as "hugger-in-buff", "fish and scrunchions", "house bankin" and "Dutch Mess". To freshen the fish and remove the salt, soak in several changes of cold water (from 8-24 hours). Simmer the desalted fish in fresh water for 20 minutes and then drain in a collander.

1 pound	salt cod bits	.5kg
1/2 cup	salt pork, diced	125mL
2	large onions	2
1 tablespoon	vinegar	15mL
4 tablespoons	evaporated milk	60mL

1. Freshen cod as described above.
2. While cod bits are cooking fry the salt pork until brown.
3. Add the chopped onion and cook until transparent. Add vinegar and milk and bring to the boiling point. Pour mixture over the cod. Serve with boiled potatoes and mashed turnip.

Yield: 6 servings

COD FISH CAKES

> There was taken and exported from this place Last year 1200 quintals of Cod Fish, besides a considerable quantity consumed by the settlers, most of which fish were taken in Log canoes and Small Boats. There undoubtedly will be four times that quantity taken this year as the Settlers will not be necessarily employed in Building.

Samuel Goldsbury to Edward Winslow, Edinburgh, N.S., 1785.[2]

1 pound	cooked salt cod	.5kg
1/4 cup	salt pork, diced	50mL
1	large onion	1
3 cups	mashed potatoes	750mL
1/2 teaspoon	dry mustard	2mL
1	egg	1

74

1. Freshen and cook the cod as described above. Fry the salt pork.
2. Chop and saute the onion. Mix all the ingredients together and form into small patties.
3. Fry in a small amount of oil until brown and crusty on one side. Once the crust is well formed it is easy to turn for browning the other side.

Yield: 4-6 servings

St. George's Day.

THOMAS MALLARD,

INTENDS to prepare a DINNER on Saint George's Day being the 23d inflant for fuch Gentlemen as may choofe to celebrate the fame at a Britons houfe.—DINNER to be on the Table at 4 o'clock:

☞ Thofe Gentlemen who wifh to meet and Dine at his houfe on that day will be pleafed to leave their names on or before the 12th of this inft.

Royal Gazette and New Brunswick Advertiser, April 3, 1787

Mallard's Inn was a popular meeting and dining place for the Loyalist's of St. John, New Brunswick. Anne Mallard carried on the business after her husband suddenly died. *The Royal Gazette and New Brunswick Advertiser* refers to dinner parties and Masonic celebrations which were held at Mrs. Mallards Tavern. Kedgeree, crimped salmon, jugged hare, "fifteen tongues served with a faggot of shallots," pork dishes and boiled puddings were favourite fare.

KEDGEREE

| 1 pound | smoked salmon or smoked cod | .5kg |

1 1/3 cups	long grain rice	325mL
2 cups	milk	500mL
4	hard cooked eggs	4
1/2 cup	32% cream	125mL
1/4 cup	butter	50mL
3 tablespoons	fresh minced parsley	45mL
1/2 teaspoon	curry powder	2mL
	salt and pepper	

1. Cook rice in salted water. Drain and rinse under running water.
2. Set a double boiler over boiling water, put the milk in the top of the double boiler. Cut the salmon in 3 or 4 pieces, place in the milk and poach until it just flakes with a fork. Transfer the salmon to a platter and skin, debone and flake.
3. Add the cooked rice, the flaked salmon, the chopped eggs, butter, cream, and 2 tablespoons of parsley to the milk. Season with salt and pepper. Add the curry and cover and cook over the boiling water until heated through. Serve on toast and garnish with the remaining parsley.

Yield: 4-5 servings

Variation: Regular cooked flaked fish can be substituted for the smoked fish.

STEAMED SALMON LOAF

Steaming, a common method of food preparation in Loyalist times, is seldom used to-day. This flavourful loaf, which is prepared ahead of time and chilled in the refrigerator, proves steaming is a method which is due for a revival.

1 pound can	red salmon	439g
2 tablespoons	lemon juice	30mL
1 teaspoon	dry mustard	5mL
1 teaspoon	worcestershire sauce	5mL
2 tablespoons	minced onion	30mL
1/2 cup	minced celery	125mL
1/3 cup	minced parsley	75mL
1/2 teaspoon	salt	2mL
dash	pepper	dash
1 1/2 cups	crushed cracker crumbs	375mL
2	eggs	2
1/2 cup	milk	125mL

76

1. Drain salmon; flake. Mix salmon liquid with lemon juice; add to flaked salmon. Blend in mustard, worcestershire sauce, onion, celery, parsley, salt and pepper.
2. Add crumbs, beaten eggs and milk. Turn into lightly greased top of a double boiler or a fish-shaped mold. Add boiling water to the bottom of the double boiler or to come half-way up the mold which is placed in a kettle. Cover and steam 1 1/2 hours.
3. Remove mold from water and place on a rack to cool. Refrigerate.

Yield: 6 servings

BAKED SALMON LOAF

Canned salmon, a staple in modern times just as a barrel of salmon was in the early days, can be used in a variety of dishes. Extra calcium is provided when the softened bones are crushed and included in recipe preparation. This loaf is great for an oven meal: baked salmon, scalloped potatoes, baked herbed carrots and a baked dessert.

1 pound can	salmon	439g
2 cups	soft bread crumbs	500mL
2	eggs, beaten	2
3/4 cup	milk	175mL
1/2 teaspoon	salt	2mL
dash	pepper	dash
1 tablespoon	onion, minced	15mL
1 teaspoon	lemon juice	5mL
1 tablespoon	butter	15mL

1. Remove any skin from the salmon; crush and use bones and juice.
2. Mix ingredients and pack in a greased loaf pan, dot with butter.
3. Bake in 350ºF (180ºC) oven for 45 minutes, or until loaf is firm and brown. Serve with lemon wedges.

Yield: 6 servings

ATLANTIC SALMON PIE

In this prize-winning recipe, the cornmeal crust combines with the salmon, cheese and olive filling to give a flavour which is sure to meet with enthusiastic response.

1 pound	canned salmon	439g
2	eggs, beaten	2
2/3 cup	chopped olives	150mL
1/2 cup	mayonaise	125mL
1 tablespoon	chili sauce	15mL
1 cup	milk	250mL
1 1/8 cup	flour	280mL
2 1/2 teaspoons	baking powder	12mL
1 teaspoon	salt	5mL
5 tablespoons	shortening	75mL
2/3 cup	corn meal	150mL
3/4 cup	cheddar cheese, grated	175mL

1. Preheat oven to 425°F (210°C). Grease a large 1.5L pie pan.
2. Remove skin and liquid from salmon — neither are used in this recipe. Mix fish with beaten eggs, olives, salt, mayonaise and chili sauce.
3. Sift flour, baking powder and salt into a bowl. Cut in shortening until it resembles coarse meal. Stir in cornmeal. Stir in milk and lightly mix until moistened. Spread dough on bottom and up the sides of the pie pan with a spoon.
4. Put salmon mixture on top of the cornmeal crust. Sprinkle with grated cheese.
5. Bake for about 30 minutes or until set.

Yield: 6 servings

SALMON GATEAU

Early recipes used interesting names and a change of herbs to provide flavour variations.

2 cups	canned or cooked salmon	439g
1 cup	mashed potatoes	250mL
1/2 cup	bread crumbs	125mL
1/2 teaspoon	salt	2mL
dash	pepper	dash
1/4 teaspoon	turmeric	1mL
1/4 teaspoon	thyme	1mL
1	egg	1
2 tablespoons	cream	30mL
1 tablespoon	butter	15mL

1. Butter a casserole dish and shake 3 tablespoons (45mL) of the crumbs around the bottom and sides.
2. Mix fish, potatoes and seasonings. Blend in eggs and cream and put in casserole. Top with the remaining crumbs; dot with butter.
3. Bake at 350°F (180°C) for 35 minutes. Turn out on a dish and serve accompanied by a fish sauce.

Yield: 6 servings

BAKED DIGBY SCALLOPS

General Timothy Ruggles in a letter to Edward Winslow Sr. dated Annapolis, N.S. July 17, 1783 described the fish available to the settlers:

> ...Fin, scale & shell fish of all kind except oysters, the want of which is richly compensated by scallops in plenty about the bigness of a common tea saucer & of excellent flavour.[3]

Fishing for the pinkish Bay of Fundy scallops was to become and still is a very important industry. The simple to prepare recipe which follows allows you to enjoy the delectable flavour and the aesthetic contrasts of golden coated scallops with the bright green parsley.

1 pound	fresh or thawed scallops	.5kg
1	egg	1
1 tablespoon	water	15mL
1/2 teaspoon	thyme	2mL
	salt and pepper	
1 cup	fine cracker crumbs	250mL
1/4 cup	fresh minced parsley	50mL
1/4 cup	melted butter	50mL

1. Always rinse and pat scallops thoroughly dry before use.
2. Beat egg with a fork, add thyme, salt and pepper and water. Dip scallops in the egg mixture, then in cracker crumbs. Arrange in a single layer in a shallow baking dish.
3. Pour melted butter over and bake in a 450°F (220°C) oven for 20 minutes. Remove from oven and sprinkle with fresh parsley. Stir lightly.
4. Serve with lemon wedges. Scallops become tough if overcooked or reheated.

Yield: 3 servings

BOILED LOBSTERS

In the 18th and 19th centuries Atlantic Lobsters were plentiful and cheap. Today they are a valuable resource and the ultimate of treats for many of us. The simplest method of preparation is again the best!

1. Fill a large deep kettle with enough water to cover the lobsters. For each quart (litre) of water add 1/4 cup (50mL) of salt. Bring to a rapid boil.
2. Grasp the lobster across the middle of the back and plunge head first into the boiling water. Use a wooden spoon to push lobster under the water.
3. When water has returned to a rapid boil reduce heat and simmer 12 minutes per pound. The feeler pulls out easily when the lobster is cooked.
4. Remove lobster and submerge under cold water to stop the cooking.
5. Prepare lobster by placing on its back and splitting lengthwise from head to tail with a sharp knife. Remove dark intestional vein that runs through the body at the centre. Discard sac or "lady" behind the head. Crack the claws. The green tamale, and red roe are considered delicacies and should not be discarded.
6. Serve lobster hot with melted butter and/or mayonaise or cold with mayonaise.

CLAM FRITTERS

Fritters of all kinds were favourite meal accompaniments in the early days of Loyalist settlements. Fresh foods such as clams, or fruits, or vegetables and cooked leftovers such as chopped fish or meats were popular ingredients.

2	eggs	2
2 cups	raw shucked clams	500mL
1 cup	flour	250mL
1 cup	milk	250mL
1/2 teaspoon	salt	2mL
1/4 teaspoon	pepper	1mL
1/4 cup	oil	50mL

1. Chop clams very fine. Make a batter by beating eggs. Gradually add flour, salt and pepper; add milk and then the chopped clams. Stir until well mixed.
2. Heat oil in skillet, drop batter by spoonfuls into the hot oil.

Brown, turn and brown the reverse side. Drain on paper towels and serve hot.

Yield: 16 fritters

SEAFOOD PIE

The Loyalist housewife could purchase fresh fish from vendors who rented stalls at the fresh fish market, from fishermen who sold whole fish out of their boats or from pedlars who went around "the town with small fish and lobster".

4 tablespoons	butter	60mL
1/3 cup	onion, chopped	75mL
1/3 cup	chicken broth	75mL
1/2 pound	boneless haddock	.25kg
1/2 pound	scallops	.25kg
1/2 pound	lobster or shrimp	.25kg
1 teaspoon	salt	5mL
1/4 teaspoon	thyme	1mL
	freshly ground pepper	
1/3 cup (approx.)	milk	75mL
1/3 cup	flour	75mL
2 tablespoons	chopped pimento	30mL

BISCUIT CRUST

1 1/2 cups	all purpose flour	375mL
1 tablespoon	baking powder	15mL
1/2 teaspoon	salt	2mL
6 tablespoons	butter	90mL
1/3 cup (approx.)	milk	75mL

1. Melt 1 tablespoon (15mL) of the butter in a large frying pan. Saute the onion. Add broth. Cut the fish in bite-size pieces and add to frying pan. Season with salt, pepper and thyme. Simmer just below the boiling point for 5 minutes. Lift fish with a slotted spoon and place in a buttered 1L pie pan.
2. Measure liquid remaining in the pan and add milk to make 1 3/4 cups (425mL). In a frying pan melt the remaining butter, blend in flour and liquid. Cook over medium heat, stirring constantly, until thickened. Check seasonings. Add pimento and pour sauce over the fish. Top with biscuit crust.
3. Mix dry ingredients in a bowl, cut in the butter using a pastry

81

blender. When mixture resembles bread crumbs add enough milk to form a dough. Knead gently 30 seconds and then roll into a 9 inch (23cm) circle.

4. Place crust over the fish filling, trim and flute edges. Cut steam vents in centre of crust. Bake at 425°F (220°C) for 10 minutes; reduce heat to 375°F (190°C) and bake for about 15 minutes or until crust is golden.

Yield: 6 servings

MEATS, POULTRY AND SUPPER DISHES

The store of George and Robert Ross stands in 1983, as it did in 1785, on Charlotte Lane in Shelburne, Nova Scotia. John Smith sketched the store as it appears to-day and then added some provisions which would have been unloaded in Loyalist times. A few of these provisions were barrels of pork, beef, bread, fresh limes; hogsheads of jamaican spirits and molasses; tierces of rice; baskets of salt; casks of currants and vinegar; kegs of barley, crackers and oatmeal; boxes of cheese, firkins of butter; boxes of mould candles and cases of Holland geneva.

MEATS, POULTRY AND
SUPPER DISHES

TOURTIERE OR FRENCH CANADIAN PIE

The French settlers, who arrived in the Maritimes 150 years before
the Loyalists, were the creators of this dish. Meat pies were popular
because the ingredients were commonly available in the settlements.
The Royal Bounty, or the free rations distributed to the Loyalists for
the first three years of the settlement, consisted mainly of flour and
pork.

Sour Cream Pastry

2 1/2 cups	flour	625mL
1/2 teaspoon	salt	2mL
1 cup	butter	250mL
1	egg	1
1/2 cup	sour cream	125mL

1. Sift flour and salt into a bowl. Drop the butter, cut in 1/4 inch
   (1cm) pieces, into the flour. Working quickly rub the flour and
   butter together until it is the consistency of coarse meal.
2. In a separate bowl, mix together the egg and sour cream. Stir into
   the flour and butter mixture. Work with the fingers until a soft
   ball is formed. Chill for 1 hour.

Filling

2 pounds	lean minced pork	1kg
1	large onion, chopped	1
1 teaspoon	salt	5mL
1/4 teaspoon	pepper	1mL
1	bay leaf crumbled	1
1/4 teaspoon	cloves	1mL
1/2 teaspoon	sage	2mL
1 teaspoon	savoury	5mL
1/2 teaspoon	celery salt	2mL
1 tablespoon	fresh parsley, chopped	15mL
1 cup	mashed potato	250mL
1/2 cup	boiling water	125mL

1. Mix pork, onions, seasonings and boiling water in a frying pan.
   Simmer uncovered for approximately 30 minutes, stirring

occasionally. Cool slightly, stir in the mashed potato. Check seasoning.

2. Line a 9 inch (1L) pie plate with the sour cream pastry. Fill pie shell with the meat mixture, mounding slightly in the center. Cover with pastry, seal edges and cut slits in the top to allow steam to escape.

3. Bake at 425°F (210°C) for 15 minutes. Reduce heat to 375°F (190°C) and bake about 30 minutes more or until crust is golden.

Yield: 6 servings

Royal American Gazette, April 25, 1785.

STUFFED PORK TENDERLOIN

2	pork tenderloins	2
	salt and pepper	
1	small onion, chopped	1
1/4 cup	oil	50mL
4 slices	white bread crumbled	4
2	parsley sprigs	2
4 slices	bacon, cut in half	4

1. Cut a deep slit in each tenderloin and lay one flat in a shallow baking pan.

2. Saute the onion until soft and transparent. In a bowl mix the bread crumbs, cooked onion, parsley, salt and pepper. Transfer this stuffing to the flattened tenderloin. Place the second tenderloin over the stuffing. Wrap the bacon slices around the stuffed tenderloins. Put skewers through the center if desired.
3. Bake in 350°F (180°C) oven for 45 minutes or until the meat and bacon is crisply browned. Carve in chunks and serve with hot applesauce or baked apple rings.

Servings: 3-4

STEAK AND KIDNEY PIE

This savoury pie, brought to Canada by English settlers, needs only a crisp tossed salad to make a perfect meal for a chilly day.

2 pounds	round steak	1kg
1	veal kidney or lamb kidneys	1
	fat from steak	
1 tablespoon	oil	15mL
1	large onion	1
1 1/2 cups	boiling water	375mL
	bay leaf	
1/2 teaspoon	thyme	2mL
1 1/2 teaspoons	salt	7mL
1/2 teaspoon	pepper	2mL
2 tablespoons	flour	30mL
2	large carrots	2

1. Trim fat from the steak and try out in a heavy frying pan. Chop onion and saute in the fat and oil. Remove onion from the pan with a slotted spoon.
2. Cut steak in one inch (2.5cm) cubes. Place in the fat and brown well. Return onions to the pan; add flour and seasonings and stir until brown. Slowly add the boiling water, stir and cook until the mixture has thickened.
3. Slice kidney, remove fat and tubes and add to the pan. Cover and simmer for 2 hours.
4. Add thinly sliced carrots and cook for 20 minutes longer. Cool and refrigerate overnight.
5. Next day:
Remove congealed fat and place the filling in a greased baking dish. Cover with pie crust (cutting slits in the top) or drop tea biscuit dough on top.
6. Bake in 425°F (210°C) oven for 30-45 minutes, until pastry is

golden.

Serves: 6

CORNED BEEF AND CABBAGE OR SAUERKRAUT

Corned Beef Dinner with quarters of cabbage and boiled potatoes
was a Loyalist Festival dish. Later on as the settlers became
acquainted with Lunenburg sauerkraut it became the favourite
accompaniment for the corned brisket.

3 pounds	corned beef brisket	1.5kg
2 pounds	cabbage or sauerkraut	1kg

1. Check with your butcher to see how long the brisket has been
    corned. Some require all night soaking in cold water — others
    can be cooked without soaking.
2. Put meat in pot with enough water to cover. Bring to boil, reduce
    heat and simmer for 2 1/2 to 3 hours. During the last 20 minutes
    of cooking add cabbage quarters or sauerkraut.
3. Serve boiled potatoes and mashed turnip along with the beef and
    kraut.

"Beef & Pork is produced in great abundance on the peninsula
of Nova-Scotia, more than is necessary for it's inhabitants.
Witness the quantities that were brought to us during the seige
of Boston".

Edward Winslow to Ward Chipman. Halifax, 26 April, 1784.[1]

BEEF STEW with HERB DUMPLINGS

These thistle-down dumplings can be quickly made and add the old
fashioned touch to stews.

4 tablespoons	oil	50mL
2 pounds	round steak	1kg
2 each	bay leaves, cloves,	2 each
	peppercorns	
1	garlic clove, minced	1
3	beef bouillon cubes	3
3 cups	water	750mL
3	potatoes, cubed	3
3	carrots, chunked	3
2	medium onion, chopped	2
1	parsnip, diced	1

88

1. Roll meat in seasoned flour (p. 91). Brown thoroughly in hot fat in a Dutch Oven or heavy frying pan. Add seasonings, bouillon cubes and water. Simmer for 1 1/2 to 2 hours.
2. Add vegetables and cook 15 minutes. Remove spices and drop dumplings over simmering stew. Cover tightly and continue simmering without peeking for 15 minutes. If desired, thicken gravy by mixing 3 tablespoons (45mL) each of flour, cold water and juice from stew. Stir in stew and cook until desired consistency. Serve at once or dumplings will become soggy.

HERB DUMPLINGS

1 1/2 cups	flour	375mL
3 teaspoons	baking powder	15mL
1 1/2 tablespoons	chilled shortening	22mL
2 tablespoons	finely chopped parsley	30mL
1/4 teaspoon	thyme	1mL
2/3 cup (about)	milk	150mL

1. Sift flour, baking powder and salt into mixing bowl. Cut in shortening finely; mix in parsley and thyme. Add milk lightly to make a drop batter. Drop by the tablespoon over the simmering stew. Cover tightly and simmer without peeking for 15 minutes. Serve immediately.

Yield: 8 servings

CORN CRUSTED MEAT PIE

..."did get some corn from town." Alex Huston April 24, 1778. In this recipe the corn meal adds nutrients, colour and an interesting change in texture and flavour.

1 pound	ground beef	.5kg
1/2 cup	chopped onion	125mL
1 tablespoon	oil	15mL
1 cup	tomatoes	250mL
3/4 teaspoon	salt	3mL
1/2 teaspoon	pepper	2mL
dash	cayenne pepper	dash
2 cups	kernel corn	500mL
1/2 cup	chopped mushrooms	125mL

TOPPING

1/2 cup	flour	125mL
1 1/2 teaspoons	baking powder	7mL
1 1/2 teaspoons	sugar	7mL
3/4 teaspoon	salt	3mL
1/2 cup	corn meal	125mL
1	egg	1
1/2 cup	milk	125mL
2 tablespoons	oil	30mL

1. Brown meat in oil in frying pan. Add onion and mushrooms and cook until tender. Add remaining ingredients. Heat and put in 2L casserole.
2. Prepare topping by sifting flour, baking powder, sugar and salt into a bowl. Stir in corn meal. Beat egg, milk and oil together. Add to dry ingredients. Mix until just moistened. Spread over meat. Bake in 375°F (190°C) oven for 35 to 40 minutes.

MEAT LOAF with CHILI SAUCE TOPPING

1 1/2 pounds	ground beef	.75kg
1	medium chopped onion	1
2 teaspoons	salt	10mL
1/2 teaspoon	sage	2mL
1/4 teaspoon	dry mustard	1mL
1/4 teaspoon	pepper	1mL
1 tablespoon	worcestershire sauce	15mL
2 cups	soft bread crumbs	500mL
1 cup	warm milk	250mL
2	eggs	2
1/4 cup	chili sauce	50mL
1/3 cup	fine bread crumbs	75mL

1. Mix beef, onions, and seasonings.
2. Soak bread in warm milk; add eggs and beat well. Combine with meat mixture. Form meat into a loaf. Sprinkle with dry bread crumbs.
3. Place loaf in a shallow bake pan. Cover with chili sauce. Pour 1/3 cup (75mL) boiling water around loaf. Bake at 350 F (180 C) for 1 hour.

Yield: 6 to 8 servings

11 June, 1787 Records of Special Session for the County of Shelburne p. 228.

Thomas Leonard the Clerk of the Market says that sometime about the thirteenth of May last he had information of a light weight being made use of in the Butcher's Market upon which the Defendent went to the Market and found the Stall of Uriah Bonder an Iron Weight made use of for a fourteen Pound weight that the Defendent weighed it and found it wanted Eleven Ounces of being weight, that he took the weight in his possession...the accused said they always made allowances for the deficiency of the weight....fined twenty shillings.

SEASONED FLOUR

Keep this seasoning handy for dredging meat and chicken.

2 cups	flour	500mL
1 tablespoon	salt	15mL
1 tablespoon	celery salt	15mL
1 tablespoon	pepper	15mL
2 tablespoons	dry mustard	30mL
4 tablespoons	paprika	60mL
1 tablespoon	garlic powder	15mL
1 teaspoon	ginger	5mL
1/2 teaspoon	thyme	2mL
1/2 teaspoon	basil	2mL
1/2 teaspoon	oregano	2mL

1. Sift together to blend evenly. Store in a tightly covered jar.

CRUMB COATING — Combine 1 1/2 tablespoons of Seasoned flour with 1 cup of fine bread crumbs.

Shelburne March 27, 1789

Mr. James Caine:

I wish you to dispose of the 20 Quintals of Fish Shipped by me, on the best Price you can and in return bring me one hundred w⁶ of white lead ground in oil and the Balance of the money lay out in good Sheep as they are meant to Stock a Farm let them be wholesome and strong the greatest part of them Ewes with their lambs, and only Rams necessary for the Flock. As you are a good Judge get such as you would choose for yourself On your return I would have you deliver them to W. Doutty who will be at Barrington just above the Beach & his receipt shall be sufficient

Sincerely

Facsimilie: Stephen Skinner to James Caine

ROAST STUFFED SHOULDER OF LAMB

"Good sheep", as requested by Stephen Skinner in his 1789 letter, were an important requirement in the settlements. Their wool was used for homespun coats and socks and the tallow was saved for candlemaking. Mutton was served more frequently than lamb. When describing his eating habits Booth wrote:

"Eat very moderate dinner, mutton hot, and cold, when I can get it, the latter with oil and vinegar". He later listed mutton as selling for 6 pence per pound.

5 pound	shoulder of lamb	2.5kg
1	onion	1
2 cups	dry bread crumbs	500mL
2 tablespoons	butter, melted	30mL
2 tablespoons	chopped parsley	30mL
1/2 teaspoon	salt	2mL
1/4 teaspoon	pepper	1mL
4	peeled boiled potatoes	4
1/4 teaspoon	rosemary leaves	1mL

1. Take onion, cut 3 slices and chop the remaining for the dressing. Prepare dressing by mixing bread crumbs, chopped onions, melted butter, salt, pepper, parsley and rosemary.
2. Cut a pocket in the shoulder and fill with the stuffing. Close with skewers.
3. Season lamb well with salt and pepper. Put in baking dish and top with the onion slices.
4. Bake in 325°F (165°C) oven for 2 to 2 1/2 hours. Add the potatoes 1/2 hour before the roast is finished. Turn them once during the cooking so they will be well browned.
5. Put roast on a heated platter and serve with hot mint sauce.

Yield: 8 servings

MINT SAUCE

1/4 cup	chopped mint leaves	50mL
1/2 cup	vinegar	125mL
1/4 cup	water	50mL
1/4 cup	brown sugar	50mL

1. Simmer ingredients in saucepan for 30 minutes. Do not allow to boil. Serve hot.

ROAST LEG OF LAMB

5 pound	leg of lamb	2.5kg
2	slivered garlic cloves	2
	salt and pepper	
2 teaspoons	oregano	10mL

1/3 cup	butter	75mL
1	large lemon, juiced	1
4	parsley sprigs	4
1/2 cup	water	125mL
2	onions, quartered	2
6	medium potatoes	6

1. Trim excess fat from meat and place skin side up in rack of roasting pan. Make small slits over the lamb and insert little slivers of garlic. Salt and pepper generously and sprinkle with oregano.
2. Melt butter, add parsley and lemon juice. Pour over the lamb. Bake at 425° F (210° C) for 20 minutes.
3. Reduce heat to 350° F (180° C); add water and quartered onion. Bake 40 minutes and add the potatoes which have been parboiled 10 minutes and then halved.
4. Bake until required doneness, medium rare, or for a total time of about 2 hours. Lamb has a better flavour if not overdone.
5. Let meat rest on heated platter for 15 minutes so it will carve easier. Serve on hot plates with pan juices.

LAMB MEAT LOAF AND POTTED LAMB

Two dishes in one! Potted meats were very popular in the eighteenth and nineteenth centuries.

2 pounds	ground lamb	1kg
2	large stalks celery, diced	2
2 cups	fresh grated carrots	500ml
1	diced, medium onion	1
2 cups	soft bread crumbs	500ml
1	egg, beaten	1
1/2 cup	tomato paste	125mL
1 teaspoon	salt	5mL
1 teaspoon	basil	5mL
1/2 teaspoon	rosemary	2mL
1 teaspoon	paprika	5mL
1/2 teaspoon	pepper	2mL
4	slices bacon	4

1. Combine all ingredients except the bacon. Divide in 2 portions. Press one in a well greased 1L loaf pan.
2. Press the other in a greased 1L casserole dish (preferably one

94

which is wider at the top) or press into an empty tomato can. Place sliced bacon on top.
3. Bake both pans about 45 minutes in a 325°F (165°C) oven.
4. Serve the loaf hot.
5. Cover the potted lamb in the casserole with foil and place a weight on top. Let cool to room temperature. Refrigerate overnight. The following day remove the weight. Serve as a cold entree or sliced for sandwiches. Will keep 1 week in refrigerator.

OXFORD JOHN

An eighteenth century recipe provides this interesting dish utilizing cold roast lamb.

	slices of roast lamb	
4 tablespoons	butter	50mL
4 tablespoons	chopped onion	50mL
2 tablespoons	flour	30mL
2 cups	meat stock	500mL
1/2 teaspoon	salt	2mL
1/4 teaspoon	pepper	1mL
1/4 teaspoon	mace	1mL
1/4 teaspoon	thyme	1mL
1/2	lemon, juiced	1/2

1. Melt one-half of the butter in a frying pan and saute the onion. Add the meat and heat until it begins to brown. Sprinkle on the flour and seasonings, stirring to coat the meat.
2. Gradually add the meat stock and stir until smooth and thickened. Add the remaining butter and lemon juice.
3. Serve garnished with parsley and surrounded by sippets (see recipe index).

CORNISH PASTIES

These half-moon pasties are as popular today as they were in pioneer times. Serve hot as a complete food unit or serve cold for eating pleasure at a picnic or buffet.

Pastry:

	flour	1L
4 cups	flour	1L
1/4 teaspoon	salt	1mL
1 1/2 cups	lard	375mL
1/2 cup	ice water	125mL

Filling:

1 pound	round steak, cubed	.5kg
2 cups	turnip, coarsely chopped	500mL
1 cup	onions, chopped	250mL
2 cups	potatoes, diced	500mL
1/8 teaspoon	sage	1mL
1 teaspoon	salt	5mL
1/4 teaspoon	pepper	1mL
1 tablespoon	cold water	15mL
1	egg	1

1. Pastry: Sift flour and salt together into a bowl. Cut in lard, with pastry blender, till the mixture resembles coarse crumbs. Add ice water, gradually, toss with a fork until the mixture holds together. Form into a ball and chill.
2. Prepare the filling by combining the beef, potato, turnip, onions and seasonings.
3. Divide chilled dough into 6 portions. On a lightly floured surface roll each portion of the dough into a 9 inch (23cm) circle.
4. Place about 1 cup (250mL) meat vegetable filling on 1/2 of each circle of dough; fold the pastry over the filling to make a half circle. Using tines of a fork seal the pastry edge; cut slits in the pastry for the escape of steam. Brush pastry surface with egg and water mixture.
5. Place on an ungreased baking sheet. Bake in 400°F (200°C) oven for 15 minutes. Reduce heat to 350°F (180°C) and bake 40-45 minutes longer or until filling is tender and pasties brown.

Yield: 6 servings

June 14, 1786 Special Sessions for the County of Shelburne

"Thomas Sheppard a Negro Man brought into Court Charged with Stealing two Peaces of Pork out of the Sloop *Charming Betsy*. William Broad being Sworn declares upon Oath that the two Peaces of Pork produced in Court were on board the Sloop *Charming Betsy* and belong to the said Sloop and he believes the said Thomas Sheppard stole them from on board — upon which the court were pleased to order that the said Thomas Sheppard should be sent to the House of Correction and to receive on his Enterance One Dozen Lashes on his bare Back with a Cat of Nine Tails and to be kept at hard labour for the space of Two Months". p. 52-53.

CHICKEN IN SHERRY GINGER SAUCE

Stanton and Hazard, whose business was situated on Prince William Street in St. John, frequently ran advertisements in the *Royal Gazette and New Brunswick Advertiser* for: "Old Sherry Wine by the Pipe, Jamaica Spirits by the Hhd." A pipe was a huge barrel which held 126 gallons and a hogshead held 63 gallons. In those days sherry or wine was added to recipes to tenderize the chickens which tended to be scrawny and tough due to the necessity of roaming around for food. The sherry in this contemporary recipe combines with the crystalized ginger to give a delightful flavour treat.

1/2 cup	flour	125mL
1 teaspoon	salt	5mL
1	cut up chicken OR	1
4	chicken breasts	4
1/2 cup	butter	125mL
1/2 cup	dry sherry	125mL
2 tablespoons	soya sauce	30mL
1/2 cup	finely chopped preserved ginger	125mL
2 tablespoons	lemon juice	30mL

1. Combine flour, salt and coat chicken pieces. Melt 3 tablespoons (45mL) butter in a frying pan. Add coated chicken pieces and brown on all sides. Spread chicken in a single layer on a 3L baking pan.
2. In a saucepan bring remaining butter, sherry, soya sauce, lemon juice and ginger to a boil. Pour over the chicken.
3. Bake in 375°F (190°C) oven for 45 minutes or until tender. Arrange chicken on a serving dish and top with the sauce and chopped green onion. Serve with rice and green beans amandine.

Yield: 4-6 servings

BAKED LEMON CHICKEN

1/4 cup	butter, melted	50mL
3/4 cup	flour	175mL
1/2 teaspoon	salt	2mL
1/4 teaspoon	pepper	1mL
1/4 teaspoon	paprika	1mL
1	cut up frying chicken	1

1. Heat oven to 400°F (200°C). Melt butter in 3L oblong pan.
2. Mix flour, salt, pepper and paprika. Dip chicken pieces in the

seasoned flour and put in pan in a single layer, skin side down. Bake 20 minutes. Turn and pour Lemon Sauce (recipe follows) over chicken. Bake about 30 minutes more, basting several times.

Yield: 4-6 servings

LEMON SAUCE

1/4 cup	salad oil	50mL
1/4 teaspoon	salt	1mL
1/2 teaspoon	pepper	2mL
1 teaspoon	curry powder	5mL
2 tablespoons	minced onion	30mL
2	lemons, juiced	2

Mix all ingredients and pour over partially baked chicken.

IMPERIAL CHICKEN

Names associated with royalty were very popular with the Loyalists!

1	cut up frying chicken	1
1/2 cup	melted butter	125mL
2 cups	dry bread crumbs	250mL
3/4 cup	grated parmesan cheese	175mL
1/4 cup	chopped parsley	50mL
1	clove garlic, crushed	1
2 teaspoon	salt	10mL
1/8 teaspoon	pepper	.5mL

1. Roll bread crumbs to the consistency of coarse meal. Mix in the parmesan, parsley, garlic salt and pepper.
2. Dip each chicken piece in the butter and then in crumbs. Put in a shallow baking dish, dot with butter and bake in 350°F (180°C) oven for 1 hour or until tender.

HOME CURED BACON AND HAM

My maternal grandmother, Mrs. Mary Delaney, was a Loyalist descendent who lived to be 103 years old. This is her recipe for sugar cured bacon and ham — was it delicious!

1 ounce	salt petre	28g
1 cup	salt	250mL
2 cups	sugar	500mL

2 tablespoons	cloves	30mL
2 tablespoons	allspice	30mL
2 tablespoons	cinnamon	30mL

Combine the ingredients and rub with hands into the ham and bacon each morning for three weeks. Keep in a cold place while curing.

IMPORTED from Philadelphia,
And to be S O L D by the Subfcribers,
at their Store, in George Street,
SUPERFINE Flour,
Common ditto,
Indian Meal,
Ship Bread,
White Bread in Barrels and Kegs,
Some Philadelphia Hams of a very
good Quality,
Rice, &c.
GEORGE and ROBERT ROSS
Shelburne, 21ft March, 1785.

Royal American Gazette, April 25, 1785.

BAKED HAM WITH CRANBERRY GLAZE OR APPLE GLAZE

Hams were imported from Philadelphia and Burlington and they were also cured locally. George Parker's account with Charles Whitworth's store shows that George Parker purchased 4 hams on Dec. 20th, 1784, and that Mrs. Patterson purchased 2 hams on December 24th.[2] A number of people must have enjoyed ham dinners during the Christmas festivities! Early recipes suggest basting the ham with wine, apple or cranberry juice.

Place a precooked whole or half ham, fat side up, on a rack in a shallow roasting pan. Do not cover or add water. Roast in 325°F (160°C) oven 12-15 minutes per pound (500g).

Forty minutes before ham is done remove it from the oven. Score the fat of the ham by cutting in criss-cross fashion to make large diamonds. Insert whole cloves in a few of the diamonds. Prepare cranberry glaze and brush part of it over the ham. Return to the oven and baste frequently with the remaining glaze.

CRANBERRY GLAZE

3/4 cup	cranberry juice	175mL
1/3 cup	brown sugar	75mL
1/2 teaspoon	dry mustard	5mL

1. Cook fresh cranberries to obtain the required amount of juice. Mix sugar and mustard, add the unsweetened cranberry juice. Cook over low heat until the sugar melts. Glaze ham as directed.

APPLE GLAZE

3/4 cup	red apple jelly	175mL
2 teaspoons	dry mustard	10mL
2 tablespoons	apple juice	30mL

Melt jelly over low heat. Stir in apple juice and mustard. Baste ham as directed.

VEAL GOOSE

Feb 4, 1788, — A boucher (butcher) came to buy the calf. Sold it for five dollars.   Alex Huston

Veal, veal broth and calves feet jelly were considered very "nourishing foods." The latter two along with white wine whey were commonly prescribed during illness.

An old recipe book suggests choosing a cold night for this filling dish and that it is almost as rich as goose itself. It is a delicious way to prepare a boned shoulder of veal.

boned veal shoulder
onion
butter

Bread Stuffing:

2 cups	stale cubed bread	500mL
1/4 cup	butter	50mL

100

1/4 teaspoon	salt	1mL
1/4 teaspoon	sage	1mL
1 teaspoon	chopped parsley	5mL
1/4 teaspoon	thyme	1mL
2 tablespoons	chopped onion	30mL

1. Prepare the bread dressing. Toast the bread cubes slightly before mixing.
2. Break open some pockets in the veal for the stuffing. Tie twine around to keep roast compact. Place stuffed meat in a roasting pan. Rub with butter and season with salt and pepper. Place an onion in the pan and bake in 350°F (180°C) oven. Allow 30 minutes to the pound. Baste frequently as veal has little fat.
3. Serve with applesauce.

VEAL STEAKS WITH LEMON

1 pound	veal steaks	.5kg
1 teaspoon	salt	5mL
3 tablespoons	butter	45mL
2 tablespoons	lemon juice	30mL
1/4 cup	flour	50mL
1/4 teaspoon	pepper	1mL
2 tablespoons	parsley	30mL

1. Pound the veal steaks until thin; combine flour, salt and pepper and dip steaks in this mixture.
2. Heat butter in skillet; brown veal on both sides and simmer until tender. Pour off fat; add lemon juice and parsley and carefully coat veal.
3. Serve with rice or home made noodles.

Yield: 3-4 servings

BREADED VEAL CUTLETS OR WEINER SCHNITZEL
Simple to prepare and delicious to eat!

2 pounds	veal cutlets	1kg
1/2 cup	flour	125mL
1/4 teaspoon	salt	1mL
dash	pepper	dash
1	egg	1
1 teaspoon	water	5mL

1 1/2 cups	fresh bread crumbs	375mL
3 tablespoons	butter	45mL
	lemon wedges	

1. Pound veal cutlets to thin slightly, sprinkle both sides with salt and pepper. Dredge with flour.
2. Beat egg slightly, add water, dip floured cutlets into the egg mixture and then into the bread crumbs. Let dry for 1 hour by placing breaded cutlets on a wire rack in the refrigerator. This helps the breading adhere to the cutlets during cooking.
3. Heat the butter in a skillet and saute the cutlets until golden brown on each side.
4. Serve with lemon wedges.

Yield: 6 servings

BAKED BEANS (Maritime style)

Homemade baked beans and steamed brown bread are the traditional Saturday night supper in the Maritimes. The tradition was probably started by the Loyalists who brought the custom from New England.

4 cups	beans, yellow eye or navy	.5kg
1/2 pound	salt pork or bacon slices	.25kg
1	medium whole onion	1
1 teaspoon	salt	5mL
1 teaspoon	mustard	5mL
1 cup	molasses	250mL

1. Wash beans and soak overnight. Next morning drain and place in saucepan. Cover with fresh water and heat until boiling; reduce to a simmer and cook uncovered until the skin of one will split when blown upon, about 45 minutes. Avoid boiling rapidly or stirring.
2. Drain beans, saving the water. Put onion in a bean crock or large casserole dish. Add the beans and remaining ingredients except the pork. Cover with the water. Cut pork pieces and put on the top.
3. Cover and bake for 5 or 6 hours at 300°F (150°C). Check occasionally during baking and add water as needed.
4. Serve with steamed brown bread — a bread much more delicious than its simple ingredients suggest!

Yield: 8-10 servings

MACARONI AND CHEESE

Macaroni, vermacelly and cheeses were listed in a 1782 Halifax newspaper advertisement, along with truffle, morel and exotic spices as "just imported from London".

This version is a company dish and can be prepared without the onions and mushrooms if you prefer a simpler fare.

2 cups	elbow macaroni	500mL
1/4 cup	butter	50mL
3 tablespoons	flour	45mL
1/2 teaspoon	salt	2mL
dash	pepper	dash
1/4 teaspoon	mustard	1mL
1/4 teaspoon	oregano	1mL
2 cups	milk	500mL
2 1/2 cups	grated cheese	625mL
1/4 cup	chopped onion	50mL
1 cup	sliced mushrooms	250mL
1/2 cup	bread crumbs	125mL
2 tablespoons	melted butter	30mL

1. Cook macaroni according to package directions. Drain well.
2. Saute onions and mushrooms in the butter in a saucepan. Blend in flour, mustard, oregano, salt and pepper. Slowly stir in milk and cook until slightly thickened. Add cheese and stir until melted.
3. Place macaroni and cheese sauce in layers in casserole dish. Top with bread crumbs tossed with butter.
4. Bake, uncovered at 350°F (180°C) for 30 minutes.

Yield: 6 servings

WELSH RABBIT (Welsh Rarebit)

The story goes that a Welsh chieftan, who ran out of game for his table, served his guests melted cheese on toast, explaining that is was "Welsh Rabbit". Chafing dishes were advertised for sale by Loyalist merchants and Welsh Rabbit was a favourite recipe for the chafing dish.

1 tablespoon	butter	15mL
2 cups	grated cheddar cheese	500mL
1/2 teaspoon	dry mustard	1mL
	salt and pepper to taste	
3 tablespoons	milk	45mL
1	egg, unbeaten	1

1. Melt butter in chafing dish, fondue pot or top of double boiler. Use low heat (if over water keep below the boiling point).
2. Add grated cheese, seasonings and milk. Stir until smooth. Add egg just before serving — this prevents the rabbit from being stringy.
3. Serve poured over dry toast or with sippets. (recipe follows)

Variation: SAVOURY RABBIT

Minced ham or anchovy paste is spread on the toasted bread and then the melted cheese is poured over the ham.

LOBSTER NEWBURG

Lobster, which was plentiful and inexpensive, was another popular chafing dish ingredient.

2 pounds	lobster	1kg
1/2 cup	butter	125mL
1/2 teaspoon	salt	2mL
few grains	cayenne	fg
grating	nutmeg	
3/4 cup	cereal cream or blend	175mL
3	egg yolks	3
1 tablespoon	sherry	1

1. Remove the lobster meat from the shell and cut in bite size pieces. Melt the butter in chafing dish or in top of the double boiler.
2. Add the lobster and cook 3 minutes. Put in the seasonings and cream. When heated add the slightly beaten yolks of eggs.
3. Stir until thickened, add the sherry and serve hot over fresh hot biscuits or with sippets. (recipe follows)

SIPPETS — (An 18th century recipe)

Trim the crusts from the slices of firm bread and then cut bread in small triangles. Either fry the pieces in butter until crisp or toast to golden brown under a salamander (use the broiling element).

DESSERTS

JS '83

Pure clear sugar was available in cones weighing from 10 to 55 pounds each and came wrapped in a deep purple paper of such an attractive tint it was carefully saved and soaked to supply dye for fine wool. The sugar cone was very hard and the mistress of the house used special cutters to cut it into lumps of equal size. Sugar was too expensive and the maids too clumsy to allow them to do it. Sometimes the sugar was pulverized with a pestle in a mortar. Both brown sugar and molasses were purchased in barrels. The large auger was used to remove the brown sugar from the barrel.

Sketched in the Ross Thomson Store (1785-) Shelburne, N.S. Note the crown or bull's eye glass in the store windows.

DESSERTS

"EARLIEST AMERICAN COOKIES" or SUGAR COOKIES

The first truly American cookbook was published in 1796. Its author, Amelia Simmons called herself "An American Orphan". Previous to Amelia's *American Cookery* all the available cookbooks originated in England. She introduced new terms such as "shortening" for fat and "cookies" (from the Dutch "koekje") for biscuits. The following recipe is a slight adaption of Amelia's "Earliest American Cookies". Coriander was grown in the gardens of the Loyalist settlers.

1/2 cup	butter	125mL
1 1/2 cups	sugar	375mL
2 cups	flour	500mL
1 teaspoon	baking powder	5mL
1/4 teaspoon	salt	1mL
1/3 cup	commercial sour cream	75mL
1 tablespoon	powdered coriander seed	15mL
2 tablespoons	milk	30mL

1. Cream butter; gradually add sugar beating until light and fluffy.
2. Sift flour, baking powder, salt and coriander together. Add dry ingredients alternately with the sour cream and milk, beating well after each addition.
3. Pinch off pieces of dough the size of a walnut and roll into a ball. Flatten out in circles on a greased cookie sheet by using a flat bottomed glass which is first dipped in sugar. Place cookies well apart on cookie sheet. The 2 inch (5cm) cookie will double in circumference during the baking.
4. Bake in a preheated 375° F (190° C) oven for about 15 minutes, or until edges begin to brown. Remove immediately to cooling racks.

Yield: 36 four inch cookies

OLD FASHIONED GINGER SNAPS

Gingerbread and gingersnaps were frequently taken on sea voyages. They keep well and "many persons find a highly spiced gingerbread a preventive to sea-sickness".[1]

1 cup	molasses,fancy grade	250mL
1/2 cup	shortening	125mL
2 tablespoons	brown sugar	30mL
2 1/2 cups	flour	625mL
1 teaspoon	ginger	5mL
1 teaspoon	cinnamon	5mL
1/4 teaspoon	cloves	1mL
2 teaspoons	baking soda	10mL
1/2 teaspoon	salt	5mL

1. Heat the molasses, brown sugar and shortening until melted and let cool.
2. Put in a bowl and add sifted flour, soda, salt and spices. Knead to a firm dough, adding more flour if necessary. Chill for 20 minutes or longer.
3. Roll out on a lightly floured surface to 1/4 inch (1cm) thickness.
4. Cut with 3 inch (7 cm) cutter or in fancy shapes. Bake on a greased baking sheet in 350°F (180°C) oven for 10-12 minutes. Cool on rack and store in air tight container.

Yield: 16-three inch cookies

SCOTCH SHORTBREAD

This best of shortbread recipes has two secrets. It is necessary to have a very fine granulated sugar, such as fruit or berry sugar, which is sold in 1kg boxes. If this is unavailable, take regular white sugar and use a rolling pin (or food processor) to make very fine granules. The second secret is the extra rolling and folding of the dough which creates the smooth texture of the shortbread.

1 pound	butter	500mL
1 cup	fruit sugar	250mL
4 cups	flour	1L

1. Cream butter. Add sugar, beating until light and puffy. Add sifted flour in four additions, making sure each addition is well mixed.
2. Take 1/4 of the mixture and roll out 1/4 inch (1cm) thick. Push into a ball and repeat procedure four times. Then roll out 1/4 inch thick and cut with cookie cutters or a small glass.
3. Repeat step #2 with the remaining dough. Place cookies on an ungreased cookie sheet and bake in 325°F (165°C) oven approximately 15 minutes. Watch carefully and cook until a pale golden color: do not brown.

SURPRISE COOKIES OR COMMODORES

1 cup	sugar	250mL
1/4 cup	lard	50mL
1/4 cup	butter	50mL
2	eggs	2
2 tablespoons	cream	30mL
1 teaspoon	baking soda	5mL
2 teaspoons	cream of tartar	10mL
1/4 teaspoon	nutmeg	1mL
2 3/4 cups	flour	675mL

Filling:

1 cup	chopped raisins	250mL
1/2 cup	sugar	125mL
1 teaspoon	flour	5mL
1/2 cup	hot water	125mL

1. To prepare cookie dough, cream the butter, lard and sugar. Add eggs one at a time beating well. Add cream and beat until light and puffy.
2. Sift flour, soda, cream of tartar and nutmeg into the sugar mixture. Mix. Chill for an hour or longer for ease of rolling.
3. Prepare filling by mixing sugar, flour and raisins in a small saucepan. Add the hot water and cook until slightly thickened. Cool.
4. Roll dough thin on a lightly floured surface. Cut into 2 1/2 inch (6cm) rounds. Place 1 heaping teaspoon of filling in the center of each round. Cover with another and press edges together.
5. Bake in 350ºF (180°C) oven for 20-25 minutes.

Yield: 16 double cookies

TRILBYS OR OATMEAL TURNOVERS

1 cup	butter	250mL
1 cup	sugar	250mL
2	eggs	2
2 1/2 cups	rolled oats	625mL
2 1/4 cups	flour	550mL
1 teaspoon	baking soda	5mL
1 teaspoon	cinnamon	5mL
2 tablespoons	milk	30mL

Filling:

2 cups	finely chopped dates	500mL
1/4 cup	sugar	50mL
1 cup	water	250mL

Variations: Turnovers may be filled with jam or a raisin filling

1. Stir sugar, dates and water in a saucepan. Simmer for a few minutes until thick and syrupy. Cool.
2. Cream butter and sugar; add eggs, beating until fluffy. Add rolled oats and beat well. Stir in milk. Add sifted flour baking soda and cinamon. Mix well and chill dough.
3. Roll thin on a slightly floured surface. Cut with a 2 1/2 inch (7cm) cookie cutter. Place a teaspoon of filling on the centre of each cookie. Fold over, press edges together with a fork to prevent filling from leaking out.
4. Place on greased cookie sheet and bake in 375°F (190°C) oven for 12-15 minutes.

Yield: 5 dozen

Variation: Roll dough, cut rounds and bake on a greased cookie sheet for 10-12 minutes. Place 2 cookies together with filling.

WELSH TEA COOKIES

1 cup	butter	250mL
1 cup	sugar	250mL
2	eggs	2
3 cups	flour	750mL
2 teaspoons	baking powder	30mL
1/4 teaspoon	nutmeg	1mL
1 teaspoon	milk	5mL
1 teaspoon	vanilla	5mL
1 cup	currants	250mL

1. Cream butter, add sugar and beat until fluffy. Add eggs one at a time beating well after each addition. Sift flour, baking powder and nutmeg into the mixture. Use a wooden spoon to complete mixing.
2. Add the milk, flavouring and currants and mix well.
3. Roll dough into balls the size of walnuts. Dip each in sugar. Place on a greased cookie sheet. Flatten with a fork.

4. Bake in 350°F (180°C) oven for 15 minutes.

Yield: 4 1/2 dozen cookies

STUFFED DATE LEMON CREAMS

Sweetmeats which were pretty bite-sized delicacies were always offered after meals. They included candied fruits, nuts or flowers.

2 cups	pitted dates	375g
1	egg white	1
2 teaspoons	lemon juice	10mL
2 teaspoons	lemon rind	10mL
2 cups	icing sugar	500mL

1. Beat the egg white and add lemon rind and juice. Mix in the sugar until a paste is formed. Fill each date generously and top with a second date.

Yield: 4 dozen filled sweetmeats

CANDIED ROSE PETALS

Serve these sweetmeats at the end of a summer luncheon or save them for a wintry day. My son-in-law collected some beautiful wild roses for me to test this procedure. Some petals were candied and others were dried and mixed with sugar to use as a flavouring.

Each rose petal has to be treated individually so only prepare a small quantity at a time. Wash the petals carefully with cold water and leave on a paper towel to dry. Blend an egg white and a small quantity of water in a small bowl. Fill a second saucer with white sugar. Coat petals with egg white and then place on sugar. Use a fork to make sure petal is well covered. Remove and place on dry towels. The next day repeat the coating and drying process. Leave until petals are crisp and then store in tightly covered container. Serve as a confection or use to decorate cakes.

Thomas Coattam, the master of one of the first Shelburne grammar schools, "had a rope he could fling with unerring accuracy at a boy and make him bring it to him and then flog him. Mrs. Coattam used to give the victims gingerbread and cookies."[2]

PRIZE-WINNING GINGERBREAD

1/2 cup	sugar	125mL

1/2 cup	butter	125mL
1	egg	1
1 cup	table molasses	250mL
2 1/2 cups	flour	625mL
1 1/2 teaspoons	soda	7mL
1 teaspoon	ginger	5mL
1/2 teaspoon	cloves	2mL
1 teaspoon	cinnamon	5mL
1/2 teaspoon	salt	2mL
1 cup	hot water	250mL

1. Cream butter and sugar. Add beaten egg and molasses.
2. Sift dry ingredients together and add. Mix well.
3. Add hot water and beat until smooth.
4. Bake in a greased 2L pan (square) for 35 minutes at 350°F (180°C).

CARROT NUT CAKE

2 cups	sugar	500mL
1 cup	oil	250mL
4	eggs	4
2 cups	flour	500mL
2 teaspoons	baking powder	10mL
1 teaspoon	baking soda	5mL
1 teaspoon	salt	5mL
2 teaspoons	cinnamon	10mL
1 teaspoon	nutmeg	5mL
3 cups	grated, raw carrot	750mL
1 cup	chopped walnuts	250mL

1. Add sugar gradually to the oil and beat until light.
2. Add eggs one at a time beating well. Stir in the sifted dry ingredients and combine thoroughly. Add carrots and walnuts. Mix well.
3. Put in a greased 4L (13x9) pan. Bake in 350°F (180°C) oven for 1 hour.

EXCELLENT POUND CAKE

Mrs. H. sent me pudding yesterday and Pound Cake excellently made a few days before that — and a fine vinegar today — some salad yesterday.

Captain William Booth, Monday, May 11, 1789.

The secret for creating an "excellently made" fine-textured pound cake is in the beating. Cream the butter well and then add the sugar very gradually while continuously beating. An electric beater is almost essential to achieve the required consistency. In Loyalist times, hickory rods were used as beaters. Some recipes suggested 30 minutes of beating!

4 cups	sifted all purpose flour	1 L
1 teaspoon	baking powder	5mL
1/2 teaspoon	salt	2mL
dash	grated nutmeg	dash
3 cups	sugar	750mL
2 cups	butter	500mL
6	large eggs	6
1 cup	milk	250mL
2 teaspoon	vanilla	10mL
1 teaspoon	lemon rind	5mL

1. The butter, eggs and milk should all be at room temperature. Sift together the flour, baking powder, salt and nutmeg. Set aside.
2. Cream the butter until very light and fluffy. Add the sugar gradually, about 2 tbsp. (30mL) at the time. Beat until the consistency of whipped cream.
3. Add eggs, one at a time, beating after each addition. Combine milk and flavouring. Add the sifted dry ingredients alternately with the milk, beginning and ending with flour. Do this in four additions with the mixer at low speed.
4. Oil and flour a large 3L tube pan. Put the cake batter into the pan. Bake at 300°F (150°C) for about 80 minutes or until the cake begins to pull away from the sides of the pan. Cool upright on a rack for 10 minutes and then invert and remove pan. Cool.
5. Serve plain or cover with an almond paste and a butter icing.

ENGLISH WEDDING CAKE

Joanna White, who was born in Shelburne in 1787 was married at a gala affair nineteen years later. Her wedding cakes consisted of 28 pounds of Plum Cake and 10 1/2 pounds of Plain Cake.[3]

2 1/4 cups	brown sugar	550mL
2 cups	butter	500mL
8	eggs	8
4 cups	flour	1L
4 cups	currants	1L

113

2 cups	sultana raisins	500mL
3/4 cup	whole mixed peel	175mL
1/2 cup	ground almonds	125mL
1/2 cup	rum	125mL
1/2 cup	glazed cherries	125mL

1. Cut the mixed peel and the glazed cherries into slivers. Mix fruit and almonds and dredge with some of the flour.
2. In a bowl cream the butter. Add the sugar gradually and beat in eggs one at a time. Fold in the fruit and remaining flour. Add the rum.
3. Grease the traditional three sizes of cake pan. Fit with two or three layers of oiled paper. Put in the batter.
4. Bake in a preheated 275°F (135°C) oven.
   Time will vary with the size of the pan — the largest one could take three hours to bake. When the cake tests done remove from oven and let cake stand 30 minutes in the pan. Remove to a wire cooling rack, peel off the paper and let rest until cold.
5. Wrap cakes in cheesecloth which has been sprinkled with rum and cover tightly with aluminum foil. Let age in a cool place adding a little rum over a period of time.
6. Book a professional to ice your creation a few days before the wedding.

JAMAICAN RUM CAKE

"Present Prices of Provisions in Shelburne" were regularly noted in Captain William Booth's Diary. On Feb. 5, 1789 he listed "excellent rum" at 5 shillings a gallon and "rum of indifferent quality" at 4 shillings.

1 cup	mixed peel	250mL
1 cup	raisins	250mL
1 cup	currants	250mL
1 cup	glazed cherries	250mL
1 cup	prunes	250mL
1/2 cup	rum	125mL
1 cup	white sugar	250mL
2 cups	flour	500mL
1 tablespoon	baking powder	15mL
1 cup	butter	250mL
3	eggs	3

1. Grind all fruits and mix together in a large glass jar. Add the rum,

seal and let stand 2-4 weeks before making the cake.
2. Cream butter and sugar. Add well beaten eggs and mix. Sift flour and baking powder together and add. Stir in the marinated fruit.
3. Grease a 9 inch (2L) loaf pan. Place the batter in the pan and bake at 350°F (180°C) for 45 minutes.

DATE RUM CAKE

Rather than marinating fruits in advance or preparing a fruit cake which needs to ripen for improved flavour, choose this recipe which is delicious as soon as it is baked.

2 cups	chopped, pitted dates	500mL
1 cup	broken walnuts	250mL
1 1/2 cups	brown sugar	375mL
1 cup	butter	250mL
7/8 cup	boiling water	200mL
1 teaspoon	baking soda	5mL
2 tablespoons	rum	30mL
2	well beaten eggs	2
1 cup	flour	250mL

1. Place dates, walnuts, sugar and butter in a bowl. Dissolve soda in the boiling water and pour over date mixture. Stir until well mixed.
2. Add the rum and eggs. Stir in the sifted flour. Pour into a 2L tube pan which has been lined with oiled paper.
3. Bake in 350°F (180°C) oven for about 1 hour. Cool on a rack and serve plain or ice with the following frosting.

RUM FLAVOURED BUTTER ICING

1/4 cup	unsalted butter	50mL
1	egg yolk	1
1 cup	icing sugar	250mL
1 teaspoon	rum	5mL

1. Beat butter until creamy. Stir in egg yolk. Beat in sugar very gradually. Beat hard until very light and fluffy.
2. Mix in the rum. Spread on top of the cooled cake.

BAKED INDIAN PUDDING

Every early cook book has a slightly different version of Indian Pudding. The method of sweetening varied and also the name of the pudding: Hasty Pudding, Stir Pudding and even Loyalist Pudding. It was told that some families had 365 Indian puddings a year.

"Though seldom seen now, this delicious pudding has cheered and warmed winter appetites through the years. It might share the oven with a meat casserole or stew...."[4]

1/3 cup	corn meal	75mL
1 cup	cold water	250mL
2 cups	scalded milk	500mL
3 tablespoons	butter	45mL
1/2 cup	brown sugar	125mL
2	eggs, beaten	2
1 teaspoon	cinnamon	5mL
1/2 teaspoon	salt	2mL
1/2 teaspoon	ginger	2mL
1/4 teaspoon	cloves	1mL
dash	nutmeg	dash
1/2 cup	molasses, fancy grade	125mL
1 cup	cold milk	250mL
1/4 cup	raisins	50mL

1. Stir corn meal in cold water, add scalded milk and butter.
2. Mix brown sugar, salt and spices and add to the corn meal mixture. Pour into a buttered 2L casserole dish.
3. Stir in eggs, molasses and raisins. Pour cold milk over the pudding. (The traditional pudding has a whey which separates out if the milk is added after the pudding is mixed).
4. Set casserole in a pan of hot water in a 350°F (180°C) oven for 2 hours.
   Serve warm with ice cream or hard sauce.

Serves: 6

ROLLED APPLE DUMPLINGS

According to folk-lore, King George III's favourite dessert was apple dumplings.

1 1/2 cups	flour	375mL
2 teaspoons	baking powder	10mL

1/2 teaspoon	salt	2mL
2 tablespoons	lard	30mL
2 tablespoons	butter	30mL
1/2 cup	cold water	125mL
1/2 cup	brown sugar	125mL
1/4 teaspoon	nutmeg	1mL
1/2 teaspoon	cinnamon	2mL
2 cups	chopped apples	500mL

1. Sift flour, baking powder and salt into a bowl. Cut in lard and butter with a pastry blender until consistency of coarse meal.
2. With a fork stir in water to make a soft dough. Turn dough on floured surface and knead *lightly* 3 or 4 times. Roll dough to a 1/2 inch (1cm) thick rectangle.
3. Sprinkle with apple, sugar and spices. Roll up like a jelly roll, cut in pieces about 2 inches (5cm) wide and stand on end in a casserole dish. Pour part of the Vanilla Sauce on them and bake in a 400°F (200°C) oven for about 25 minutes.
4. Pour the remaining sauce over the dumplings when served.

VANILLA SAUCE

1/2 cup	white sugar	125mL
2 tablespoons	flour	30mL
2 tablespoons	butter	30mL
1 cup	water	250mL
1 teaspoon	vanilla	5mL

1. Mix flour, sugar and water. Cook until thick, stirring continuously.
2. Remove from heat Add butter and vanilla.

BLUEBERRY BUCKLE

Blueberry Buckle, a sort of three-layered cobbler, is best made with fresh blueberries or those frozen whole (unthawed).

1/4 cup	butter	50mL
1/2 cup	white sugar	125mL
1	egg	1
2 cups	flour	500mL
2 teaspoons	baking powder	10mL
1/4 teaspoon	salt	1mL

| 1/2 cup | milk | 125mL |
| 2 cups | blueberries | 500mL |

Topping

1/4 cup	butter	50mL
1/2 cup	brown sugar	125mL
1/3 cup	flour	75mL
1 teaspoon	cinnamon	5mL

1. Cream butter and sugar until light; beat in egg. Sift together flour, baking powder and salt and mix in alternately with the milk, beginning and ending with dry ingredients.
2. Spread batter across bottom of a well greased 9x5x3 (2L) baking dish. Cover with blueberries.
3. For the topping: Mix sugar, cinnamon and flour. Cut in butter until mixture is crumbly. Sprinkle on top of blueberries.
4. Bake in 375°F (190°C) oven for 35-45 minutes or until buckle is puffed and golden brown. Cool and then cut in squares. Serve warm.

Yield: 8-10 servings

EVE'S PUDDING

Here are two recipes for Eve's pudding. The first one is for your reading enjoyment and the second one for your eating enjoyment!

EVE'S PUDDING 1

If you want a good pudding, mind what you are taught
Take eggs six in number, when bought for a groat;
The fruit with which Eve her husband did cozen,
Well pared, and well chopped, at least half a dozen
Six ounces of bread, let Moll eat the crust,
And crumble the rest as fine as the dust;
Six ounces of currants, from the stem you must sort,
Lest you break out your teeth, and spoil all the sport
Six ounces of sugar won't make it too sweet,
Some salt and some nutmeg will make it complete
Three hours let it boil without any flutter,
But Adam won't like it without wine and butter.

Anonymous

118

EVE'S PUDDING 2 (simply delicious)

4 cups	dried or fresh apples	1L
3 tablespoons	butter	45mL
1/4 cup	flour	50mL
1 1/2 cups	milk	375mL
2 tablespoons	sugar	30mL
1/2 teaspoon	nutmeg	2mL
1/2 teaspoon	vanilla	2mL
2	eggs, separated	2

1. Peel, slice and put fresh apples in a saucepan with 1/4 cup (50mL) water. Cover and simmer 10 minutes. If using dried apples rehydrate in water. Place stewed apples in the bottom of a greased pie plate.
2. Melt butter in a saucepan; stir in flour and add milk a little at a time. Cook until a smooth thick sauce. Pour sauce into a bowl, blend in sugar and nutmeg. Add the beaten egg yolks and vanilla. Fold in stiffly beaten egg whites. Pour mixture over the apples and bake in 350°F (180°C) oven for 30 minutes or until set.

CRANBERRY APPLE CRUNCH

2 cups	fresh cranberries	500mL
3 cups	apples, cored, sliced	750mL
3/4 cup	white sugar	175mL
1 1/2 cups	rolled oats	375mL
3/4 cup	brown sugar	175mL
1/2 cup	melted butter	125mL

1. Combine apples, cranberries, and white sugar in an oblong dish (10x6 or 1.5L).
2. Mix rolled oats, brown sugar and melted butter. Sprinkle over the fruit mixture. Bake at 350ºF (180ºC) about 1 hour.
3. Serve warm or cold.

Yield: 6 servings

CRANBERRY UPSIDE DOWN CAKE

2 cups	fresh cranberries	500mL
2/3 cup	sugar	150mL
1/3 cup	water	75mL

1 1/4 cup	pastry flour	300mL
3/4 cup	sugar	175mL
2 teaspoons	baking powder	10mL
1/3 cup	butter	75mL
1/2 cup	milk	125mL
1 teaspoon	vanilla	5mL
1	egg	1

1. Place cranberries, sugar and water in a small saucepan and boil for 3 minutes. Remove from heat and spread cranberries and syrup evenly in an oblong (10x6 or 1.5L) pan.
2. Sift flour, baking powder and sugar into a mixing bowl. Cut in butter with a pastry blender. Add milk and vanilla. Mix well. Add egg. Beat. Drop this mixture on top of the cranberries.
3. Bake at 350°F (180°C) for 30-35 minutes. Cut in squares and invert when placing on serving dishes.

Yield: 6 servings

STEAMED CHRISTMAS CARROT PUDDING

This recipe was used by the early settlers for many festive occasions. It is a light textured pudding and is my family's favourite Christmas dessert.

1 1/2 cups	flour	375mL
1 cup	brown sugar	250mL
1 cup	suet, finely chopped	250mL
1 cup	raisins	250mL
1 cup	currants	250mL
1 cup	grated carrots	250mL
1 cup	grated potatoes	250mL
1 teaspoon	baking soda	5mL
1 teaspoon	salt	5mL

1. Mix and sift dry ingredients, add suet and fruit; add vegetables and stir until well blended. Steam for 3 hours. Serve with Vanilla Sauce and Hard Sauce.

To Steam Pudding

The easiest way: Grease the top part of a double boiler and fill 2/3 full with batter. Cover with the lid, place one inch of water in the
120

bottom part of pan and simmer. It will be necessary to replenish the water occasionally.

The traditional way: Grease a crockery pudding bowl or a pudding mold. Fill 2/3 full and cover tightly with aluminum foil tied over the top. Place the mold on a rack in a large kettle. Add water to reach one half the way up the sides of the mold, and steam the pudding, with the lid on the kettle for the required time.

VANILLA SAUCE

2 cups	boiling water	500mL
1 cup	sugar	250mL
2 tablespoons	flour	30mL
2 tablespoons	butter	30mL
1 1/2 teaspoons	vanilla	7mL
1/4 teaspoon	nutmeg	1mL

1. Combine flour, sugar and nutmeg in a small saucepan; slowly add the boiling water. Simmer for 5 to 8 minutes, stirring constantly.
2. Add butter and stir until melted. Remove from heat. Add vanilla and transfer to a pitcher for serving.

HARD SAUCE

1/3 cup	butter	75mL
1 1/4 cups	icing sugar	300mL
1/2 teaspoon	vanilla	2mL
1/4 teaspoon	nutmeg	1mL

1. Cream the butter; add the sifted sugar gradually, beating until it is light and creamy. Add the vanilla and beat again.
2. Put in a small attractive serving dish and sprinkle with nutmeg. Cover with saran wrap and put in refrigerator to harden.

QUEEN of PUDDINGS or PRINCESS PUDDING

A very glamourous bread pudding which merits its continuous popularity.

3 cups	cubed stale bread	750mL
4 cups	milk	1L
2 tablespoons	butter	30mL

3/4 cup	sugar	175mL
4	eggs, separated	4
1	grated lemon rind and juice	1
1/2 cup	red current jelly	125mL
1/4 cup	white sugar	50mL

1. Soak crumbs in milk for 5 minutes. Cream butter, stir in sugar, beaten egg yolks and lemon rind. Stir in soaked bread crumbs.
2. Turn into a greased 1.5 L oblong dish. Place in a pan of hot water and bake in 350°F (180°C) oven for 35 minutes or until set. Spread jelly over the top. Beat whites until stiff, fold in sugar and lemon juice. Swirl on top of the jelly. Bake in 325°F (165°C) oven for about 25 minutes or until lightly browned.

Yield: 8 servings

ORANGE MERINGUE PUDDING

1 tablespoon	cornstarch	15mL
1/2 cup	sugar	125mL
3	eggs, separated	3
1 cup	milk	250mL
4	oranges	4
2 tablespoons	sugar	30mL

1. Mix the sugar and cornstarch, stir in the beaten egg yolks. Place in a heavy saucepan, add milk and cook, while stirring, until thick.
2. Peel, seed and cut oranges in small pieces. Place in bottom of a casserole dish. Add the thickened custard sauce.
3. Make a meringue by stiffly beating the egg whites, add sugar and then pile on top of the pudding. Bake in 350°F (180°C) oven until delicately browned. Cool to room temperature and serve.

Yield: 4 servings

CREAMY RICE PUDDING

Another old fashioned stand-by. Long slow cooking is necessary for development of creaminess and flavour.

| 1 cup | whole grain rice | 250mL |
| 2 | eggs, beaten | 2 |

2 cups	milk	500mL
1/3 cup	brown sugar	75mL
1/3 cup	raisins	75mL
1/2 teaspoon	salt	2mL
1/4 teaspoon	nutmeg	1mL

1. Put rice in 2 cups (500mL) of salted water; bring to a boil; cover; turn off heat and let stand for 15 minutes. Drain rice, rinse under cold water and drain again.
2. Beat eggs in a bowl. Add sugar, raisins, nutmeg, milk, salt and cooked rice. Transfer to a casserole dish.
3. Place in a pan of hot water and bake in 325°F (165°C) oven for 1 1/2 hours. Stir once after cooking for 30 minutes to remove the film. Serve with a dash of nutmeg on top or with maple syrup or a caramel sauce.

CARAMEL GINGER SAUCE

Delicious with vanilla ice cream, rice pudding or cottage pudding.

1 1/4 cups	hot water	300mL
2 cups	sugar	500mL
3 tablespoons	chopped candied ginger	45mL

1. In a large frypan brown the sugar, stirring constantly over medium heat. Add hot water. Stir until smooth, about 4 minutes. Add ginger. Cool and serve.

RASPBERRY FLUMMERY

As soon as the land was cleared of trees raspberry plants shot up and provided fruit of excellent flavour. The berries were used to make a favourite drink, raspberry vinegar, and for deserts such as syllabub and flummery.

1/4 cup	sugar	50mL
1/4 cup	cornstarch	50mL
3 cups	milk	750mL
1	egg yolk, beaten	1
2 teaspoons	vanilla	10mL
2 cups	raspberries	500mL

1. Combine sugar and cornstarch in a saucepan. Blend in milk. Cook and stir over low heat until the mixture thickens and

123

bubbles.
2. Stir a small amount of the hot sauce into the egg yolk. Return to the pan and cook 2 minutes longer. Remove from heat and add vanilla.
3. Pour into a serving bowl. Cover with plastic wrap and chill for at least 2 hours. Arrange raspberries attractively on top before serving.

Yield: 6 servings

STRAWBERRY SHORTCAKE

Banquets celebrating patron saints and birthdays of royalty were a frequent occurrence in Loyalist times. After the main courses were removed from the table a variety of desserts would be formally arranged around an elaborate centrepiece.

| 5-6 cups | fresh strawberries | 1.5L |
| 1/2 cup | sugar | 125mL |

Shortcake:

2 cups	flour	500mL
3 teaspoons	baking powder	15mL
1/2 teaspoon	salt	2mL
2 tablespoons	sugar	30mL
1/2 cup	butter	125mL
1	egg, lightly beaten	1
1/2 cup (about)	milk	125mL

1. Wash, hull and quarter berries. Place in a large bowl, cover with sugar and let stand several hours at room temperature. Just before serving crush with a potato masher.
2. Shortcake: Sift flour, baking powder, sugar and salt into a bowl cut in butter, with a pastry blender, until the mixture resembles coarse meal. Add egg, stir and add enough milk to make a dough. Spread on an ungreased baking sheet and shape into a rectangle about 1/2 inch (1.5cm) thick.
3. Bake the shortcake at 425°F (210°C) for 12 minutes or until golden brown. Cool before cutting.
4. Cut shortcake into large squares. Split, fill with crushed berries, pile more berries on top. Garnish with whipped cream.

Yield: 6 shortcakes

CHOCOLATE BLANC MANGE

By 1786 a "chocolate manufactory" had been established at the corner of Prince William and St. James Streets in St. John. Both wholesale and retail chocolate were available and a few bags of cocoa.

Here's a good tasting dessert without eggs — a bonus in pioneer days when the hens were not laying and a bonus to-day when low cholesterol diets are advocated. Skim or 2% milk can be used.

3/4 cup	white sugar	175mL
3 tablespoons	flour	45mL
3 tablespoons	cornstarch	45mL
3 tablespoons	cocoa	45mL
4 cups	scalded milk	1L
1 teaspoon	vanilla	5mL
1 tablespoon	butter	15mL

1. Combine sugar, flour, cornstarch and cocoa in the top of a double boiler. Add the scalded milk and steam for 1 hour.
2. Remove from heat, add butter stir in and then add vanilla.
3. Serve cold either plain or with whipped cream.

Yield: 6 servings

ORANGE FOOL

Fool, an old English dessert composed of custard and stewed fruit, was popular throughout the settlements. One version combined sieved gooseberries and custard, another variation used rhubarb.

3	eggs, beaten	3
1 cup	cereal cream	250mL
1 teaspoon	grated orange rind	5mL
3/4 cup	orange juice	175mL
2 tablespoons	sugar	30mL
1/4 teaspoon	nutmeg	1mL
1 teaspoon	butter	5mL

1. Beat eggs, add cream, orange juice and rind, sugar and nutmeg. Put in a saucepan and cook over low heat until mixture coats a metal spoon. The custard should be stirred during the cooking.

Remove from heat and add the butter, stirring until it has melted. Put in serving dishes and chill.

Yield: 4 servings

APPLE CRISP

In the Annapolis Valley there are a few 300 year old apple trees — evidence of the suitability of soil and climate to fruit farming. Apple crisp provides a favourite fruit under a crispy butterscotch crust. The rolled oats increase the nutrients and flavour.

5 cups	sliced, pared apples	1.25L
1/4 cup	sugar	50mL
1 teaspoon	cinnamon	5mL
2 teaspoons	lemon juice	10mL
2 tablespoons	water	30mL
1/4 cup	butter	50mL
1/3 cup	brown sugar	75mL
1/3 cup	flour	75mL
3/4 cup	rolled oats	175mL

1. Grease a 1.5L baking dish. Prepare apples and place in a baking dish. Sprinkle with sugar and cinnamon. Combine lemon juice and water. Pour over the apples.
2. Cream butter, gradually add brown sugar. Blend in oats and flour. Sprinkle over the apples.
3. Bake in 375°F (180°C) oven for about 35 minutes.

Yield: 6 servings

APPLE PAN DOWDY

Old cook books have many dishes with interesting names apparently names were given just for the fun of saying them.

5 cups	sliced, pared apples	1.25L
1 cup	firmly packed brown sugar	250mL
1/4 cup	flour	50mL
1 cup	boiling water	250mL
1/4 cup	molasses	50mL
1 tablespoon	lemon juice	15mL
1 tablespoon	butter	15mL
1 teaspoon	vanilla	5mL
1 teaspoon	cinnamon	5mL
1/2 teaspoon	nutmeg	2mL

Topping:

1 cup	flour	250mL
1/2 teaspoon	salt	5mL
2 teaspoons	baking powder	10mL
3 tablespoons	butter	45mL
1/2 cup	milk	125mL

1. Pare, core and slice the apples. Place in a greased 2L baking dish. Combine the brown sugar and flour. Place in a saucepan, stir in water and molasses and cook until thickened. Add butter, vanilla, cinnamon, nutmeg and lemon juice. Pour over the apples.
2. Prepare the topping by sifting flour, baking powder and salt into a bowl. Cut in the butter using a pastry blender. Add milk and stir only until blended. Drop the batter by spoonfuls on top of the apples.
3. Bake at 400°F (200°C) for 35 minutes. Serve warm.

Yield: 8 servings

APPLE ALMOND DESSERT

Base:

1 cup	flour	250mL
2 tablespoons	brown sugar	30mL
1/3 cup	butter, softened	75mL

Filling:

2 cups	sliced pared apples	500mL
1/2 cup	white sugar	125mL
1 tablespoon	butter, melted	15mL
2 tablespoons	lemon juice	30mL
1/2 teaspoon	grated lemon rind	2mL
1	egg, beaten	1

Topping:

3/4 cup	packed brown sugar	175mL
1 tablespoon	soft butter	15mL
1	egg, beaten	1
1/2 cup	chopped almonds	125mL

127

1. Prepare the base by creaming the butter, sugar and flour. Press into a 1 L square baking pan.
2. Prepare filling by melting 1 tablespoon (15mL) butter in a skillet. Add the white sugar, lemon juice, lemon rind and apples. Stir and heat gently until the apples are translucent.
3. Remove apples from the heat and cool slightly. Beat the egg and add apple mixture to the egg. Transfer to the prepared base. Spread evenly.
4. Prepare the topping by creaming butter and sugar, add egg and almonds. Drop over the apple mixture as evenly as possible.
5. Bake at 350°F (180°C) for 30 minutes or until firm and golden brown. Cool in pan. Cut and serve.

Yield: 4-6 servings.

APPLE OATMEAL BARS

A delicious way to add fiber to your diet.

Oat Base and Topping:

1 3/4 cup	rolled oats	425mL
1 1/2 cups	flour	375mL
3/4 cup	butter	175mL
1/4 teaspoon	soda	1mL
1 cup	brown sugar	250mL
1 teaspoon	salt	5mL

Filling:

2 1/2 cups	sliced apples	625mL
2 tablespoons	butter	30mL
1/2 cup	white sugar	125mL
1 teaspoon	cinnamon	5mL

1. Cream butter and sugar in a bowl. Mix in oats, flour, soda and salt. Press one-half of the mixture into a 1.5L oblong baking dish.
2. Cover with the filling. Add remaining oat mixture. Press down with a wooden spoon.
3. Bake at 325°F (165°C) about 45 minutes. Cut in squares and serve warm or cold.

Yield: 18 bars

NEVER FAIL PASTRY

5 cups	flour	1.25L
1 teaspoon	baking powder	5mL
1 tablespoon	brown sugar	15mL
3/4 teaspoon	salt	3mL
1 pound	lard	.5kg
2/3 cup	water	150mL
2 tablespoons	vinegar	30mL
1	unbeaten egg	1

1. Sift flour, baking powder, salt and sugar into a bowl. Chop fat into flour mixture.
2. Beat egg slightly in measuring cup. Fill cup with water until the egg and water measure 3/4 cup (175mL). Add vinegar. Add egg, water and vinegar to flour and fat mixture and mix. Chill.
3. This may be kept in refrigerator for a week to ten days.

Yield: 4 pies

FOR SALE,

TWELVE Hundred acres of LAND, in the townfhip of *Prince-William*, allow'd to be equal, if not fuperior to any on the river St. John, confifting of one hundred and ninety-two rods front ; near ninety arces of it are interval, thirty of which is fit for cultivation ; two fmall dwelling houfes, and feventy grafted fruit trees. Alfo, a Negro man and woman, flaves, and three good milch Cows ; the whole to be difpofed of for eighteen hundred dollars.—For particulars enquire of Capt. *Stewart,* on the premifes.
Feb. 26th, 1786.

Royal Gazette and New Brunswick Advertiser, Feb. 28, 1786.

The preceding 1786 advertisement illustrates how industriously the Loyalists worked at clearing lands and building homes. Grafted fruit trees began to bear fruit three years from the planting. A variety of early and later bearing trees assured a continuous supply of fruit during the summer and fall. Some fruit was stored in barrels in root cellars, others were preserved in syrup or dried. A "paring bee" was a fun time when young male and female friends got together and pared, cored, sliced and strung the fruit which then hung from the kitchen rafters until thoroughly dried.

APPLE PIE

5 to 6 cups	sliced apples	1.5L
1/2 cup	brown sugar	125mL
3 tablespoons	flour	45mL
1 teaspoon	cinnamon	5mL
1/4 teaspoon	nutmeg	1mL
1 tablespoon	lemon juice	15mL
	pastry for 2 crust pie	

1. Heat oven to 425°F (210°C). Prepare pastry and line a large pie plate.
2. Peel, core and thinly slice apples and put in lined pan. Add apples piling them higher in the centre. Mix flour, sugar, nutmeg and cinnamon together. Sprinkle over the apples. Sprinkle lemon juice over — increase amount if apples are not tart.
3. Cover with top crust. Seal and flute edges. Slit top and cover edge with a narrow strip of aluminum foil to prevent burning. Remove foil during the last 15 minutes of baking.
4. Bake in 425°F (210°C) oven for 20 minutes, reduce heat to 350° and bake about another 25 minutes. The crust should be golden and the juice should begin to bubble through the slits before it is removed from the oven.

PUMPKIN PIE

Pumpkin and corn were the first seeds to be planted among the stumps on the settlers cleared land. A frequently quoted old verse goes:

> "For pottage, and puddings, and custards, and pies,
> Our pumpkins and parsnips are our common supplies.
> We have pumpkins at morning and pumpkins at noon;
> If it were not for pumpkins, we should be undoon."

1 1/2 cups	stewed or canned pumpkin	375mL
1 cup	evaporated milk, undiluted	250mL
2	eggs	2
1 cup	brown sugar	250mL
1 teaspoon	cinnamon	5mL
1/2 teaspoon	cloves	2mL
1/4 teaspoon	nutmeg	1mL
1 teaspoon	ginger	5mL
2 tablespoons	molasses	30mL

1. Mix dry ingredients. Beat eggs, add milk. Combine all ingredients. Pour in unbaked pie shell.
2. Bake at 425°F (210°C) for 50 minutes or until a knife inserted 1 inch (3cm) from the sides will come out clean. The centre may look soft but will set later.

RHUBARB CUSTARD PIE

Rhubarb, which was sometimes called Pie Plant, continues to provide a refreshing spring-time delight.

3	eggs	3
3 tablespoons	milk	45mL
2 cups	sugar	500mL
4 tablespoons	flour	60mL
3/4 teaspoon	nutmeg	3mL
4 cups	rhubarb, diced	1L
1 tablespoon	butter	15mL

1. Prepare pastry. Line a 1L pie pan with pastry.
2. Beat eggs, add milk. Combine flour, sugar and nutmeg. Stir into the egg mixture. Mix in rhubarb. Place in the pie plate. Dot with butter and cover with lattice top.
3. Bake in 400°F (200°C) oven for 1 hour or until nicely browned. Serve warm.

OLD-FASHIONED LEMON PIE

An easy way to prepare an all time favourite.

1 cup	sugar	250mL
1 tablespoon	cornstarch	15mL
1 tablespoon	flour	15mL
3	eggs	3
1/4 cup	melted butter	50mL
	Juice and rind of two lemons	

| 1/4 cup | milk | 50mL |
| 1 | unbaked crust (no roll pastry) | 1 |

1. Mix dry ingredients in a bowl.
2. Add butter, beaten eggs, lemon juice, lemon rind and milk.
3. Pour into unbaked pie shell and bake at 375°F for 35 minutes.

NO-ROLL PASTRY

1 1/2 cup	sifted all-purpose flour	375mL
1 1/2 teaspoons	sugar	7mL
3/4 teaspoon	salt	3mL
1/2 cup	vegetable oil	125mL
3 tablespoons	cold milk	45mL

1. Prepare and press into pie pan as directed. Sift flour, sugar and salt into pie pan. Combine cooking oil and milk in measuring cup. Beat with fork until creamy, pour all at once into centre of flour mixture, mix with fork until flour is completely dampened. Set aside about 1/3 of the dough for topping.
2. Press evenly and firmly with the fingers to line bottom and sides of pan, pressing dough to uniform thickness. Fill with desired filling, crumble remaining dough with fingers into small bits. Sprinkle over filling.
3. Bake in hot oven, 400°F (200°C) for 15 minutes. Reduce heat to 350°F (180°C) and bake 30 to 40 minutes or until crust is brown and filling is done. This amount makes one single shell and is also very nice for tart shells.

FRESH GOOSEBERRY PIE

A day before she landed at St. John and a month before her daughter Hannah was born Sarah Frost wrote in her diary:

Our people went on shore and brought on board spruce and gooseberries, and grass and pea vines with blossoms on them, all of which grow wild here.[5]

Wild gooseberries apparently grew abundantly in most areas of the Maritimes. A number of the islands which dot the coastlines are called Gooseberry Island and nearby inhabitants still visit them each August to gather the fruit for making distinctive pies, jams, jellies and wine.

4 cups	gooseberries	1L
1 cup	white sugar	250mL
2 tablespoons	flour	30mL

1 tablespoon	butter	15mL
dash	mace	dash
2 crust	pastry	2

1. Snip off stem and blossom ends of berries. Wash and drain.
2. Mix flour, sugar and mace thoroughly and stir in berries.
3. Line pie pan with pastry. Add the fruit and cover with a lattice top. Dot the butter between the lattice.
4. Bake at 425°F (220°C) for 35 to 45 minutes. Serve warm topped with whipped cream.

PLUM (CHERRY, PEACH, WILD STRAWBERRY) PIE

This recipe comes from Miss Beecher's 1859 cook book. The deep colour of the "in season fruit" and the distinctive flavour of whichever fruit you choose to use makes this a rave dessert. To "extend" the fruit and still create a delicious pie combine apples and plums or use strawberries with some fresh rhubarb.

Line your dish with paste. After picking over and washing fruit carefully (peaches must be pared, and the rest picked from the stem), place a layer of fruit and a layer of sugar in your dish, until it is well filled, then cover it with paste, and trim the edge neatly, and prick the cover. Fruit pies require about an hour in a thoroughly heated oven.

Royal Gazette and *New Brunswick Advertiser* Sept. 5, 1786.

VEGETABLES

VEGETABLES

Vegetable Plants, herbs and seeds available in Shelburne, N.S. 1785-1820:

Aniseed

Angelica

Apple

Asparagus

Balm

Basil — Sweet

Beans — English
    scarlet runner
    bush
    pole
    mixed kidney
    broad Windsor
    yellow dwarf kidney
    early mazagan
    white Canterbury
    large white
    black eyed dwarf
    toker
    black speckled dwarf
    red speckled dwarf
    large pod
    white battersea
    Dutch runners
    early yellow
    hotspur
    dwarf marrows
    horse
    early negra
    mumfords
    yellow speckled
    early hotspur

Beets — white
    red

green

Broccoli — large late
    late purple
    early purple
    large green
    curled green
    curled brown

Cabbage — early sugar loaf
    savory cabbage
    early cabbage
    large cabbage
    early battersea
    wrench's dwarf
    early York
    early Dutch
    hollow drum head
    green savoy (curled)
    yellow savoy (curled)
    large battersea
    deep red
    early yorkshire
    heart shaped
    Imperial
    red Dutch
    flat Dutch
    broglio
    Russia
    scotch cattle

Chammomile

Caraway

Carrots — early horn
    long orange
    red
    orange

137

Catnip

Cauliflower — early
            large
            late

Celery — upright
         solid

Cherry

Convolvulus minor

Coriander

Corn salad

Cress — curled
        garden

Cucumbers — long prickly
            green turkey
            short prickly
            long green turkey
            white spine
            southgate
            spanish

Endive — green curled
         broad leafed
         battersea
         white
         curled
         Batavia
         early curled

Feverfew, Featherfew

Fennel — Sweet

Garlic

Gooseberry

Grass — pepper
German Greens
Hawthorne — English

Hemp — Russia

Hyssop

Kale — Scotch
       Brown

Lavatera — mallow

Lavender

Leek

Lettuce — cabbage
          hardy green
          tennis ball
          green Silesia
          green cross
          white cross
          Brown Dutch
          Capuchin
          Bull and Button
          Royal Brown Dutch
          imperial
          grand admiral
          Drumhead
          Egyptian

Love Apple

Marjoram — sweet
           pot

Melon — Italian
        fine catelope
        Roman
        musk

Mint

Mustard — Black
          white
          brown

Nasturtiums

Onions — Deptford
         White Spanish
         Blood red
         Strasburg
         Silver skin
         Madiera
         reading
         Welch
         London

Orris — white

Parsley — Hamburgh
curled
common

Parsnip — common

Peach

Pear

Pea — green garden
early
marrowfat
large marrowfat
dwarf English
golden hotspur
Imperial
black eye'd
large egg
Charlton
Dwarf marrow
early frame
early hotspur
Boundivale
Royal Oak
Glory of England
Dutch Sugar dwarf
Wrench's late dwarf

Peppermint

Plum — green gage

Poppy

Potato — English white
Blond
Blue

Pumpkin

Purslane

Quince

Radish — short top
salmon
turnip
salad
early short top

spanish
long top
red turnip
early purple
scarlet salmon
black spanish

Rhubarb

Rose — Damascena

Rue

Sage

Savory — summer
winter

Spinach — round
prickly

Squash

Strawberry

Thyme

Trefoil

Turnip — early stone
French
mixed field
best winter
yellow Aberdeen
white globe
red seed
purple seed
large yellow Aberdeen
red topp'd
White Norfolk
Lapland
early white
early Dutch
green
Yorkfield

CRUSTY PIONEER POTATOES

"...as soon as the danger of freezing is over send a Barrel of Seed Potatoes as be mentioned by Maria who seldom omits reminding me when the articles of potatoes are in question."

Stephen Skinner to Peter Mackie   Feb. 27, 1789

8	small potatoes	8
1/2 cup	butter, melted	125mL
1 cup	dry bread crumbs	250mL
1/2 teaspoon	sugar	2mL
1/2 teaspoon	cinnamon	2mL

1. Cook potatoes and drain well.
2. Combine bread crumbs, sugar, cinnamon and butter in a mixing bowl. Transfer mixture to a paper bag; add potatoes and shake bag to coat.
3. Arrange in the bottom of an ungreased casserole dish. Bake in 350°F (180°C) oven for 30 minutes.

Yield: 4-6 servings

SCALLOPED POTATOES

"Walking this afternoon I saw Parson Rowland — I spoke to him; he was employing his people in planting potatoes — setting them in hills, which he says answers best; he tried them every way in Rhode Island, where he lived last, and found that method was best."

Captain William Booth   May 12, 1789.

4	potatoes, pared	4
	salt and pepper	
	flour	
	milk	
1 tablespoon	butter	15mL
1 tablespoon	onion, minced	15mL

1. Slice potatoes thinly and put a layer in a greased casserole dish. Sprinkle with salt, pepper, and flour. Dot with 1/2 the butter and 1/2 the onion.
2. Repeat the layers. Add milk until it shows through the top layer.
3. Cover and bake 350°F (180°C) for 1 1/4 hours. Uncover and bake 15 minutes longer.

140

Yield: 4-6 servings.

Variation: POTATOES SCALLOPED WITH HAM: Place 1 cup (250mL) of cubed cooked ham in bottom of casserole, add potatoes, onions, flour and top with another 1 cup (250mL) of ham and continue as above.

BAKED POTATO TURNIP PUFF

Alexander Huston's 1787 diary has an annotated list at the back of his potato plantings and harvesting. The month of April was spent preparing the ground and hoeing. During May and June he planted 9 bushels and by the end of October had dug 80 bushels.

2 cups	hot mashed potatoes	500mL
2 cups	hot mashed turnip	500mL
2 tablespoons	melted butter	30mL
1/2 teaspoon	salt	2mL
1/8 teaspoon	pepper	1mL
2 tablespoons	light cream	30mL
1	egg, well beaten	1

1. Mix potato and turnip; add other ingredients in the order given.
2. Put in a well greased casserole dish and bake at 400°F (180°C) for 20 minutes. Serve piping hot.

Yield: 6 servings

BROCCOLI WITH HOLLANDAISE SAUCE

Six varieties of broccoli seeds were available for planting in the "garden lotts". "Early" and "late" varieties allowed harvesting over a longer period of time.

Wash broccoli well under running water. Trim coarse leaves and woody part of stem. Cut lengthwise in serving size pieces. Place upright in saucepan. Add boiling water to 1 inch (3cm) level. Return quickly to the boil and cook until tender crisp (10-25 minutes depending on maturity). Drain well and serve.

HOLLANDAISE SAUCE

3	egg yolks	3
1/2 cup	melted butter	125mL
1 tablespoon	lemon juice	15mL

1. Beat egg yolks in top of double boiler with a wooden spoon. Beat in melted butter, a little at a time, add lemon juice. Place over simmering water. Stir and cook until thickened (4 to 5 min). Immediately remove from heat.
2. Set aside until ready to reheat over hot water. Serve.

CRISPED PARSNIPS

An old cookbook claims: "A delicious vegetable; so good that my family forgets manners and eats this with their fingers like candy".

Scrape the parsnips and boil until tender crisp. Allow to cool; then cut in long slices about one-third of an inch thick. Season with salt and pepper. Dip in melted butter and flour. Place 2 tablespoons (30mL) of butter in frying pan. When hot add parsnips and cook until golden brown. Serve hot.

CAULIFLOWER au GRATIN

"...I wish to make my compliments to Judge Lee of Cambridge and ask him for a few Garden Seeds of cauliflower if possible".

Stephen Skinner to John Innman, April 23, 1789.

Trim outer leaves and stem from cauliflower. Soak head for 15 minutes in 1 quart (1L) of water with 2 tablespoons (25mL) of salt. Separate into flowerets and place in saucepan. Add 1 cup (250mL) of boiling water and cook until tender crisp (10-15 minutes). Drain and serve with cheese sauce.

CHEESE SAUCE

2 tablespoons	butter	30mL
2 tablespoons	flour	30mL
1/2 teaspoon	salt	2mL
1/2 teaspoon	mustard	2mL
dash	paprika	dash
dash	cayenne	dash
1 1/4 cups	milk	300mL
1 cup	cheese, grated	250mL

1. Melt butter, blend in flour and seasonings. Gradually add milk. Stir and cook until smooth and thick.
2. Add cheese and stir until melted. Serve at once or keep warm in
142

top of double boiler.

PUMPKIN FRITTERS

Pumpkins are good for much more than the traditional Thanksgiving Pies and Hallowe'en Jack-o-Lanterns. In fact, when the jack-o-lantern is finished, use it in one of the early pumpkin recipes.

2	egg whites	2
2 tablespoons	flour	30mL
1/2 teaspoon	salt	2mL
1/2 teaspoon	cinnamon	2mL
1	lemon, juiced	1
	thin slices of raw pumpkin	
3 tablespoons	butter	45mL

1. Marinate pumpkin slices in lemon juice.
2. Prepare batter by beating egg whites until frothy, blend in the flour, cinnamon and salt, and beat until smooth.
3. Dip pumpkin slices in the batter and fry in the butter until golden brown. Drain on paper towels. If desired sprinkle with white sugar. Serve while hot.

GOURMET BARLEY CASSEROLE

May 8, 1788 "Sowing Bald Barley...In the afternoon preparing ground for potatoes". Alex Huston

Barley was a popular grain with the pioneers because it grew well and when eaten in bread or broths provided a sensation of repletion. This attractive casserole makes an interesting change at dinner parties from rice and potatoes.

1/3 cup	butter	75mL
2	medium onions	2
1 1/2 cups	fresh mushrooms	375mL
1 1/2 cups	pearl barley	375mL
3	pimentos	3
3 cups	chicken stock or bouillon cube broth salt and pepper	750mL

1. Melt butter in a frying pan. Saute coarsely chopped onions and sliced mushrooms. Add barley and cook until barley is a delicate brown, stirring frequently.

143

2. Transfer mixture to a buttered casserole. Pour in chicken broth. Add salt and pepper. Place coarsely chopped pimentos on top. Cover and bake at 350ºF (180ºC) for about 60 minutes, or until barley is tender and liquid is absorbed.

Yield: 8 servings

STUFFED MUSHROOMS

Wild mushrooms were gathered for current use during the spring and summer. The favoured ketchup was made from mushrooms and some were pickled for use in winter months.

24	large mushrooms	24
1/4 cup	butter	50mL
1/2 cup	chopped onion	125mL
3/4 teaspoon	salt	3mL
1/4 teaspoon	pepper	1mL
3 tablespoons	grated parmesan cheese	45mL
1 tablespoon	bread crumbs	15mL

1. Wash and dry mushrooms. Remove the stems and chop fine.
2. Melt butter in a frying pan and saute onions and chopped stems for 5 minutes. Mix in salt, pepper, bread crumbs and cheese.
3. Stuff the mushrooms with the mixture. Place in a greased baking dish. Bake at 375ºF (190ºC) for 15 minutes.

Yield: 6 servings

MUSHROOM PASTIES

The appearance of mushrooms after an early spring rain were a welcome sight. These pasties can be served as a hot hors doeuvre or as part of a vegetarian meal.

1	large onion	1
1/3 cup	butter	75mL
4 cups	chopped mushrooms	1L
1 teaspoon	thyme	5mL
1 teaspoon	salt	5mL
1/2 cup	chopped parsley	125mL
3/4 cup	celery	175mL
	pastry (double crust)	

1. Saute onion in butter. Add mushrooms, celery, salt and thyme. Simmer until vegies are tender crisp. Add parsley. Let cool while

144

preparing the pastry.
2. For hors doeuvres: Cut 2 1/2 inch (4cm) circles of pastry. Put a rounded tablespoon of filling on each, fold over and seal edge with a fork.
For main course pasties: Cut 5 inch (13cm) circles. Place filling on half of circle, fold over and seal edges by crimping with a fork.
3. Cut slits in pasties to allow steam to escape. Bake on ungreased cookie sheet in 350°F (180°C) until golden.

Yield: 6 servings

HODGE PODGE

A dinner of new vegetables and what a treat!

Take small new potatoes, peas, string beans, carrots and onions, or any combination of new vegetables from the garden. Prepare and then cook in just enough water to prevent burning. Cook the vegetables together, starting with those which require the longest cooking period and adding the others so they will be cooked at the same time. Add 2 tablespoons (30mL) of butter, 1 cup cream (250mL), season to taste with salt and pepper. Serve hot.

SUCCOTASH

In summer fresh beans and corn and in winter dried beans and corn were used to prepare this dish which originated with the Native Indians. The Indian name is "m'sickquatash" — "maize not ground or crushed".

2 pounds	young green beans	1kg
3 slices	salt pork or bacon	3
12	ears of corn	12
	salt and pepper	
1 cup	cream (optional)	250mL

1. Rinse green beans in cold water and break in 1 inch (3cm) pieces. Place in a saucepan with bacon pieces. Add 1/2 cup of water and simmer 10-12 minutes. Cut the kernels from the cob and add to the beans. Cook about 10 minutes longer, or until beans and corn are tender. Remove salt pork or bacon. Add butter, salt and pepper and heated cream. Serve. If cream is not used serve with extra butter.

SPINACH WITH ROSEMARY

An intriguing vegetable herb combination

1 pound	fresh spinach	.5kg
1/2 teaspoon	crushed rosemary	2mL
1 tablespoon	chopped parsley	15mL
1 tablespoon	chopped green onion	15mL
2 tablespoons	butter	30mL
	salt and pepper	

1. Melt butter in a heavy saucepan. Add onion and parsley.
2. Wash spinach until clean. Tear it coarsely and place in saucepan with butter; add rosemary. Cover, bring to the boiling point; reduce to simmer and cook about 8 minutes. Serve immediately.

CORN OYSTERS

These fritters were served hot for breakfast or as a vegetable at dinner. They make a great addition to a vegetarian meal.

1/2 cup	flour	125mL
1/2 teaspoon	baking powder	2mL
1/2 teaspoon	salt	2mL
1 cup	canned corn or fresh corn kernels	250mL
1	egg, separated	1
2 tablespoons	melted butter	30mL
1 tablespoon	milk	15mL

1. Sift dry ingredients. Combine beaten egg yolk, corn milk and butter and add to dry ingredients. Fold in stiffly beaten egg white.
2. Drop from a spoon into hot fat in a skillet. Cook until brown on one side, turn and brown the other. Serve hot, plain or with maple syrup.

Yield: 16 oysters

EARLY GARDEN PEAS WITH FRESH MINT

1 pound	fresh peas	.5kg
1/8 inch	boiling water	1cm
1 teaspoon	chopped fresh mint	5mL

1. Hull peas. Cook covered in heavy saucepan with the boiling water until tender. Drain; fold in mint and serve with light cream and butter.

TOASTED PUMPKIN SEEDS

pumpkin seeds
butter

1. Wash pumpkin seeds to remove any membrane. Spread seeds from pumpkin on a cookie sheet to dry. This takes about 2 days. Measure.
2. Dot each cup of pumpkin seeds with 3 tablespoons (45mL) butter. Place in 375°F (190°C) oven and toast for 7 minutes. Shake pan frequently.
3. When golden brown place the toasted seeds on paper towels to drain.
4. Store in a airtight container.

CARROTS VICHY

"The carrots were remarkable fine last season though not equal the ones at home. Pease turned out indifferent. Beans were very good."

Captain William Booth, March 18, 1789.

3 cups	small carrots	750mL
1/2 cup	boiling water	125mL
1/2	fresh lemon, juiced	1/2
3 tablespoons	melted butter	45mL
2 teaspoons	minced parsley	10mL

1. Scrape carrots and chop into chunks. Cook, covered, in saucepan with boiling water and lemon juice. Do not overcook.
2. Drain carrots and dry off any remaining liquid over low heat. Add melted butter and saute until carrots are lightly brown. Toss with minced parsley and serve.

VINAIGRETTE DRESSING (True French Salad Dressing)

Nothing compares to this simplest salad dressing, providing you use a first-rate oil and vinegar. It also makes an excellent marinade for meats.

147

2 tablespoons	wine vinegar	30mL
6 tablespoons	olive or vegetable oil	90mL
1/2 teaspoon	salt	2mL
1/4 teaspoon	freshly ground pepper	1mL

Skake ingredients vigorously in a jar with a tight lid.

Yield: 1/2 cup

MUSTARD VINAIGRETTE: Add 1/4 teaspoon (1mL) dry mustard to the basic dressing.

HERBED VINAIGRETTE: Add 1 tablespoon (15mL) of chopped fresh herbs — basil, chives, dill, marjoram, parsley or tarragon — or 1 teaspoon (5mL) dried herbs to the basic mixture.

Yield: 1/2 cup (125mL)

CREAM SALAD DRESSING

This dressing puts the finishing touch to a luscious fresh fruit salad.

2	egg yolks	2
2 tablespoons	vinegar	30mL
1 tablespoon	sugar	15mL
2 tablespoons	butter	30mL
1/2 teaspoon	salt	2mL
dash	cayenne pepper	dash
1/2 teaspoon	mustard	2mL
1 cup	whipped cream	250mL

1. Beat egg yolks until light; add vinegar slowly, sugar, butter and seasonings. Cook over hot water until thick and smooth.
2. Beat in whipped cream just before serving.

Yield: 1 cup (250mL)

MAYONNAISE

1	egg	1
1 teaspoon	dry mustard	5mL
1 teaspoon	salt	5mL
3 tablespoons	vinegar	45mL
2 cups	vegetable oil	500mL

1. Beat egg, add mustard and salt.
2. Add oil *slowly*, beating *continuously* with a rotary beater. If the oil is added a few drops at a time and the beating is continuous an emulsion will form and the mixture become thick and glossy.
3. Add the vinegar 1 tablespoon (15mL) at a time. Beat a few seconds and refrigerate.

FOOD PROCESSOR METHOD. Mix egg, mustard, salt and vinegar. Add oil, letting it slowly run down the spout, while the processor is running and the metal blade whisking. This method takes seconds.

BOILED SALAD DRESSING

2 tablespoons	flour	30mL
1 tablespoon	sugar	15mL
1 teaspoon	dry mustard	5mL
1/2 teaspoon	salt	2mL
2	egg yolks	2
2 tablespoons	butter, softened	30mL
3/4 cup	milk	175mL
1/4 cup	vinegar	50mL

1. Mix dry ingredients in top of a double boiler. Add egg yolks and mix well. Add butter and blend. Add a small amount of the milk and stir until smooth. Place the pan over the boiling water and slowly add, while stirring, the rest of the milk.
2. When well blended add the vinegar and cook until thickened. Remove from heat and store in a covered container in the refrigerator.

This dressing is excellent for potato salad.

CHARTREUSE:* A PRETTY DISH OF VEGETABLES

An old manuscript recipe was the source of this very attractive, good-tasting vegetable dish and to think the ingredients are inexpensive root vegetables!

4	small diameter carrots, cut in this slices (round)	4
1/2	medium sized turnip cut in short julienne strips	1/2
4	potatoes, sliced in chunks	4
	salt and pepper	
	light cream	
	butter and fresh chopped parsley	

1. Cook each vegetable in a separate saucepan with a small amount of boiling water until each vegetable is tender crisp.
2. Arrange vegetables in a shallow round oven to table dish or in a pyrex pie plate by placing the carrots and turnips alternately in an attractive pattern around the edge of the dish.
3. Mash the potatoes, season with salt and pepper and add enough light cream for a good consistency. Fill the center of the dish with the mashed potatoes. Dot the top of the vegetables with butter.
4. Bake in 350^{0}F (180^{0}C) oven until heated through. Serve with a light parsley garnish.

Yield: 6 servings

* See glossary.

GLOSSARY

andirons: metal supports for wood at the front of the hearth. Also supported the drip pan when using a spit.

ashcakes: cornmeal bread wrapped in cabbage leaves and baked in hot ashes.

barm: homemade yeast which was kept in a scoured stone jar in a cool place.

bladder: usually from a pig was tied on the mouth of a jar containing preserved foods to keep the food fresh.

calves-foot broth: made by boiling calves feet in water; cooling and then removing the fat; adding salt and nutmeg "and if approved a spoonful of good wine". This broth was a must "for the sick".

calves-foot jelly: the chilled broth was also used for gelatine.

caudle: a hot wine drink made with rice gruel, eggs, sugar, nutmeg and wine.

chartreuse: the "queen of entrees" characterized by an arrangement with a central mould or mound surrounded by a variety of vegetables arranged in orderly rows.

comfit: sweetmeats made of sugared or brandied roots and seeds.

corned beef: name derived from the "corns" of salt petre used for pickling the meat.

cow-heels: a clear jelly "is very useful to keep in the house, being a great improvement to soups and gravies". (1807)

dutch oven: a three-legged iron pot that stood over the coals and had a flanged lid on which coals could be heaped.

faggot: a small bunch of parsley, thyme and bay leaf tied up — or a bunch of shallots.

firkin: a small wooden cask or vessel which held 56 pounds of butter. A firkin is larger at the bottom than at the top and was made of wide staves. It was also a beer measure — four firkins of beer equalled one barrel.

flummery: dessert of fruit, cream and wine.

fool: a cold, sweet, creamy custard.

151

gammon: ham

gill: a measure equal to 1/2 cup.

gridiron: metal grid on legs used for searing and cooking small pieces of fish directly over the coals.

hair sieve or **tammy**: was made of horse hair and an essential kitchen utensil for straining soups and sauces.

hoecakes: cornmeal bread cooked on a hoe blade over the fire.

hogshead: large barrel holding 130-150 gallons of molasses.

isinglass: was prepared from the swimming bladders of sturgeons and when melted yielded a high quality gelatine.

jacks: various gadgets used to turn the spits (clocks, pulleys, weights and even smoke)

ketchup: a great variety are found in early cookbooks: anchovy, lobster, oyster, mushroom, lemon and in later years tomato.

lug poles: of wood or iron were built in the fireplace wall to provide a rack from which the cooking pots were suspended.

marbles: "boiled in custard, or anything likely to burn will by shaking it in saucepan prevent it from catching." (1807)

marrow scoup: small six inch scoup used to remove the marrow from bones. Marrow was considered a delicacy.

mortar and pestle: most common household ones were made of white wedgewood or wood. They were used to grind sugar, herbs and spices.

nasturtium seeds: were pickled and used as a substitute for capers.

pearlash: an early form of baking powder obtained from wood ashes. Boiling water was poured through the ashes and the resulting lye was strained through coarse linen cloth into a large iron pot. This was placed over a hot fire and evaporated to a black powder. It was then purified by calcination and re-crystalized into "pearl-ash". Large quantities were exported to Europe.

pease: the early name for "peas".

peel: long handled wooden paddles used to place and remove food baked in a brick oven.

pipkin or posnet: a small wooden bucket with one stave longer than the other to serve as a handle. It was used for dipping from a tub.

152

porringers: dishes made of cast iron, pewter or silver and used to warm small quantities of food.

posset: a hot drink consisting of ale, milk, spices and bread crumbs.

potted: cooked meats, fish or cheese as packed tightly in earthenware pots and sealed with clarified butter.

powdering tub: a large container in which meats were powdered (covered with salt) to preserve them.

pudding cloth: used to boil the traditional puddings. Old cookbooks emphasized the cloth should be dipped in boiling water, squeezed dry and floured each time it was used in order to have a fine flavoured pudding.

quintal: wooden box which held 100 pounds of dried fish such as cod.

Q.S.: abbreviation used in old recipes which means "quantam sufficit", that is, to taste.

ratafia: almond essense used as an ingredient in puddings and sweet meats.

reflector oven: or bird oven, or tin kitchen was open on the side facing the fire. It was made of sheet metal and the shiny surface of the curved side farthest from the fire reflected the heat which hastened the cooking of birds and meat. It was scoured with sand to keep it shiny.

removes: food removed from the dining tables between courses and replaced by others: pigeon pie replaced by stuffed whole salmon.

rose hips: used for tea and jam thus providing Vitamin C and preventing scurvy.

rye 'n' Injun: bread made from rye flour and corn meal.

salamander: a long handled round flat disk of iron or other metal which was heated in the fire until it glowed and then passed quickly over a dish to brown the topping. Probably got its name from the mythical lizard-like salamander which was supposed to live in the fire. Some chefs still use a salamander.

saleratus: an early form of baking soda.

sallet: salad

sippets: small pieces of bread fried in butter.

snow: fresh clean snow was used to replace eggs in some recipes when eggs were scarce or expensive.

souse: pickled foods such as herring-baked in a vinegar sauce.

153

spaddle: "for stirring butter and eggs together nothing is better than a spaddle. It should be about a foot long, and flattened at the end like a mush-stick, only broader." (Miss Leslie)

spider: frying pan with a long handle and three legs to hold it above the coals.

spruce beer ads appeared regularly in the St. John, 1786 newspapers: "the excellence of the water and his thorough knowledge of the quality of spruce, from long experiences in Canada and during his residence in this place, enables him to assure them, that they may depend on his good spruce Beer as any brewed in America. Captains of vessels supplied at the shortest notice..."

suckets: candied fruit peels prepared by cooking the peel in a sugar syrup, drying and repeating the process several times.

sweetmeats: served regularly at tea time or as final course at a meal. They were small bite size sweets such as sugared fruits, nuts, rose petals or violets.

syllabub: a fancy dessert made of cream, lemon and wine and served with an elaborate garnish. A frequently quoted version: "Fill a bowl with wine and place under a cow and then milk the cow into the bowl until a fine froth has formed at the top".

tierce: used to transport wine and equal to 42 U.S. gallons.

trammel: a wrought iron gadget with slots into which pots could be hooked at various levels. Sometimes there were two hooks at the bottom which were used to hang a roast over the coals.

treacle: molasses

treenware: wooden plates or spoons.

trenchers: the earliest form of plates were made of flat pieces of wood with shallow indentations on the side to keep the sauces and gravies high from spilling. Courting couples liked to share a trencher.

trivets: three-legged brass or iron stands used to support saucepans. Sauces tended to be milk-based and required a gentle heat so the saucepan was placed on a trivet and hot ashes were heaped under it.

wine whey: frequently prescribed for the sick:
"To a pint of boiling milk put two glasses of wine;mix it, but do not boil it again; let it stand a few minutes, and strain it through a muslin bag or a very fine sieve. Sweeten it with loaf sugar". (Mrs. Cornelius, 1845)

154

FOOTNOTES

INTRODUCTION

1. MSS Diary of Captain William Booth. Volume #1.
2. *Ibid.* Volume #2.
3. *Ibid.* Volume #3.
4. *Ibid.*
5. *Ibid.*
6. *Ibid.* Volume #5.
7. *Ibid.* Volume #6.
8. Raymond, W.O. "The Founding of Shelburne". pp. 227, 236.
9. Jeffrey, R.W. (Ed.) *Dyott's Diary* p. 54.
10. Shelburne County Court Records. Reel 1, pp. 260-265.
11. Blakeley, Phyllis. "Boston King". p. 3.
12. MSS Diary of Alexander Huston.

SOUPS AND CHOWDERS

1. Neil, Miss E. *The Everyday Cook Book and Family Compendium* p. 20.
2. Leslie, Miss Eliza. *Miss Leslie's New Receipts for Cooking.* p. 16.
3. By a lady (Maria Rundell) *A New System of Domestic Cookery.* pp. 104-105.
4. Parloa, Maria. *Miss Parloa's New Cook Book and Marketing Guide.* p. 82.
5. By a lady. *A New System of Domestic Cookery.* p. 114.
6. MSS White Collection #1542, April 17, 1795.

BREADS

1. Raymond, W.O. *The Winslow Papers 1776-1828.* p. 106.

FISH

1. Raymond, W.O. *Kingston and the Loyalists of the "Spring Fleet" of 1783.* p. 29.
2. Raymond, W.O. *The Winslow Papers.* p. 270.
3. *Ibid.* p. 106.

MEATS, POULTRY AND SUPPER DISHES

1. *Ibid.* p. 190.
2. MSS White Collection #472, Vol. 949.

DESSERTS

1. Leslie, Miss Eliza, *Miss Leslie's New Receipts for Cooking.* p. 225.
2. Archibald, Mary. *Gideon White Loyalist.* p. 37.
3. *Ibid.* p. 39.
4. Abrahamson, R.A. (Ed.) *Cook Not Mod: or Patorial Cookery.* p. 67.
5. Raymond, W.O. *Kingston and the Loyalists of the "Spring Fleet" of 1783.* p. 30.

VEGETABLES

1. MSS Curatorial Report 27 "The Gardens of Shelburne Nova Scotia 1785-1820." pp. 34-39.

BIBLIOGRAPHY

Newspapers

Nova Scotia Gazette and Weekly Chronicle, Halifax, N.S. Sept. 4, 1770-March 31, 1789.

Nova Scotia Packet and General Advertiser, Shelburne, N.S. 1786- (all available issues)

Port Roseway Gazetteer and Shelburne Advertiser, Shelburne, N.S. 1784-1785 (all available issues).

Royal American Gazette, Shelburne, N.S. 1785 (all available issues).

Royal Gazette and Miscellany of the Island of St. John, Charlotte Town, July 1791-1792 (all available issues).

Royal Gazette and New Brunswick Advertiser. St. John, N.B. 1785-1800 (all available issues).

Royal Gazette and Nova Scotia Advertiser. Halifax, N.S. April 7, 1789 — December 30, 1800.

Manuscripts

Archibald, Mary. *Shelburne, Home of the Loyalists.* Shelburne Historical Society, 1978.

        — (Ed.) *United Empire Loyalist Series.* Toronto: Dunburn Press.

Booth, William. MSS *Diary of William Booth, Shelburne, N.S. 1787-1789.*

6 vol. Wolfville, N.S. Rare Book Collection, Acadia University.

Delaney, Mrs. Mary. Manuscript Cook Book (1866-1969)

Harvey, M.M. *Curatorial Report #27, N.S. Museum* "Gardens of Shelburne Nova Scotia 1785-1820." Halifax, 1975.

Huston, Alexander. *Diary of Alexander Huston 1787-1788.* Public Archives of Nova Scotia (Pans) MG1, Volume 48.

New Brunswick Historical Society. *Loyalist Souvenir, 1783-1933.* St. John N.B. 1933.

New Brunswick Museum Catalogue One. *The Loyalists.* St. John, N.B. 1975.

Nova Scotia Museum. *Domestic Life in Early Halifax.* Halifax, 1976.

Stephen Skinners *Day Book of Letters 1780-1793.* New York Historical Society Collections. 170 Central Park West, New York. on microfilm at Shelburne County Museum.

MSS White Collection 1761-1890. No. 1-1561, Public Archives of Nova Scotia.

Books

Abrahamsom, R.A. (Ed.) *Cook Not Mad; or Rational Cookery being a collection of original and selected recipes.* Kingston, Ont. 1831, reprint Toronto: Cherry Tree Press, 1973.

Abrahamson, Una, *God Bless Our Home Domestic Life in Nineteenth Century Canada.* Toronto: Burns and MacEachern Ltd. 1966.

Almanac published by C.H. Belcher, Halifax. 1866.

Archibald, Mary. *Gideon White, Loyalist.* Shelburne Historical Society, 1975.

— *Rules and Orders of the Friendly Fire Club, Shelburne, 1784.* Halifax, Petheric Press, 1982.

Bates, Christina. *Out of Old Ontario Kitchens.* Toronto: Pagurian Press, 1978.

Beeton, Isabella: *Beetons Book of Household Management.* London, 1861.

Carter, Susannah. *The Frugal Housewife.* Boston. 1772.

Chase, A.W. *Dr. Chase's Recipes.* London, Ontario: E.A. Taylor, 1867.

Church of England Institute Receipt Book. Halifax: 1888.
158

Clarke, Anne: *Surprise Cook Book.* St. Croix Soap Manufacturing Co., St. Stephen, N.B., 1899.

Cook, Maude C. *Three Meals A Day.* Chicago: The Educational Company, 1890

Cornelius, Mrs. *Young Housekeepers Friend.* Boston: Thompson, Bigelow and Brown. 1871.

Crowell, Edwin. *A History of Barrington Township and Vicinity, Shelburne County, Nova Scotia, 1604-1870.*

Earle, Alice Morse. *Home Life in Colonial Days.* Grosset & Dunlop, 1898.

Ellet, E.F. *The Practical Housekeeper and Cyclopedia of Domestic Economy.* New York: Strager and Townsend. 1857.

Hilchey, Florence. *A Treasury of N.S. Heirloom Recipes.* Halifax: Dept. of Agriculture and Marketing. 1967.

Jeffrey, R.W. (Ed.) *Dyott's Diary 1781-1845. Vol. 1 A Selection from the Journal of William Dyott, Sometime General in the British Army and Aide-de-Camp to His Majesty King George III.* London: Archibald Constable & Co. 1907.

Jewry, Mary, *Warnes Everyday Cookery.* New York: Frederick Warne & Co. 1889.

Ladies of Toronto and other cities and towns. *The Home Cook Book.* St. John, N.B. R.H. Morrow, 1877.

Leslie, Miss Eliza. *Miss Leslie's New Receipts For Cooking.* Philadelphia: TB Petersen & Brothers, 1852.

Matthews, Hazel. *The Mark of Honour.* Toronto: University of Toronto Press, 1965.

Morse, R.E. "Report on Nova Scotia by Col. Morse 1784" *Canada Archives Report 1884.*

Munroe, Rev. James. "History and Description of the Southern and Western Township of Nova Scotia in 1795". *Report of the Trustees of the Public Archives of Nova Scotia 1947.*

Murdoch, Beamish. *History of Nova Scotia or Acadie.* Halifax: James Barnes, 1867.

Neill, Miss E. *Everyday Cook Book and Family*

Compendium. Chicago: Donahue & Co. 1884.

Nightengale, Maria. *Out of Old Nova Scotia Kitchens.* N.Y.: Charles Scribner's Sons. 1971.

Parloa, Maria. *Miss Parloa's New Cook Book and Marketing Guide.* Boston: Estes & Laureat. 1880.

Phipps, Frances. *Colonial Kitchens, Their Furnishings and Their Gardens.* N.Y.: Hawthorne Books, Inc. 1972.

Raymond, W.O. "The Founding of Shelburne" in Volume VIII of the *Collections of the New Brunswick Historical Society,* St. John N.B. 1909.

— *Kingston and the Loyalists of the "Spring Fleet" of 1783.* N.B., St. John, 1889.

— *Winslow Papers AD 1776-1826.* Printed under the auspices of the New Brunswick Historical Society. St. John, N.B. 1901.

Rundel, Maria. *A New System of Domestic Cookery and Adapted to the Use of Private Families.* Boston: William Andrews, 1807.

Simmons, Amelia. *American Cookery.* Hartford: Hudson and Goodwin, 1796.

Shelburne County Sessions Court Records, 1784-1800. (Microfilm), Shelburne County Museum.

Ware, Cecilia. *English 18th Century Cookery.* Romania: Roy Bloom, Ltd. n.d.

Warren, Mrs. Jane. *The Handy Reliable Cook Book.* N.Y. Hurst & Co. 1892.

Wright, Esther Clark: *The Loyalists of New Brunswick.* Hantsport, N.S. Lancelot Press, 1955.

Young Ladies Society of First Baptist Church, Rochester, N.Y. *Mother Hubbard's Cupboard.* 1877.

Young, John. *38 Letters of Agricola on the principles of Vegetation and Tillage,* Halifax: Holland and Co. 1822.

INDEX

162

164

165